SpringerBriefs in Education

For further volumes:
http://www.springer.com/series/8914

Sabrina Leone

Characterisation of a Personal Learning Environment as a Lifelong Learning Tool

 Springer

Sabrina Leone
Università Politecnica delle Marche
Ancona, Italy

ISSN 2211-1921   ISSN 2211-193X (electronic)
ISBN 978-1-4614-6273-6   ISBN 978-1-4614-6274-3 (eBook)
DOI 10.1007/978-1-4614-6274-3
Springer New York Heidelberg Dordrecht London

Library of Congress Control Number: 2013932481

Springer is part of Springer Science+Business Media (www.springer.com)

To Giovanni and Alessandro

Preface

Motivation and problem statement

The diffusing lifelong learning (LLL) vision, emerging practices with social semantic computing technologies and research findings signal the need for more personal, social and participatory approaches that support learners in becoming active users and co-producers of learning resources, rather in gaining control over the learning process as a whole, and in pursuing personal life goals and needs. In particular, there is an increasing understanding that learning occurs for the most part outside the traditional formal situations, especially for adult lifelong learners.

Emphasis on the shift from formal to informal e-learning through knowledge management and sharing has been placed, with particular attention to Personal Learning Environments (PLE) as learner-centred spaces, against Learning Management Systems (LMS) as organisation-centred platforms that neglect individual differences and potential. Nevertheless, investigations are motivated by the numerous educational theories, implications and challenges that the concept of PLE has posed. Moreover, since research literature points out the role of scaffolding in activating higher order learning competencies (McLoughlin & Lee, 2010), in-depth studies need to be carried out about how self-regulation can be scaffolded by a PLE.

The dichotomy LMS vs PLE has been transformed into models of integration of the two in some research literature (Giovannella, 2008; Leo et al., 2010). However, the smooth integration of formal and informal learning environments for adult lifelong learners, on the background of a student-centred framework, requires an attentive design of the underlying technological architecture. Indeed, this change in perspective towards student-centred technology-enhanced learning environments has brought about a rethinking of knowledge, knowledge management, teaching and learning, networks and the individual. Information overload, diversity and distribution highlight the necessity for content and infrastructure applications to interoperate and exchange data in order to better support lifelong learners' and educators' needs. Personalisation, trustworthiness and assessment on the collection of resources are actual research issues.

In relation to personalisation of learning, LMSs, the formal learning component of the integrated environment, are weak. Educational and psychological theories argue that learners have different ways in which they prefer to learn, and that students with a strong preference for a specific learning style may have difficulties in learning if the teaching approach mismatches it (Felder & Silverman, 1988; Felder & Soloman, 1997). On this basis, models for the detection of learners' learning styles need to be evaluated, and adaptive educational systems that could be integrated in a LMS need to be investigated.

Finally, trustworthiness and assessment on the collection of resources call for a thorough analysis of suitable Social Semantic Web tools to be adopted within the integrated learning environment.

Research issues

The aim of this research is to devise and validate a format, that is a plan for the organisation and arrangement of a specified learning path, for the characterisation of adult lifelong learners' PLEs. In order to realise this goal, investigations regarding three research questions have been conducted:

1. How do adult lifelong learners learn?

The provision of a suitable format for the characterisation of PLEs requires a sound knowledge of lifelong learners' characteristics and learning profiles, first. In this work, European Union (EU) reports about LLL policies and achievements, and relevant research literature have informed the development of the *SSW4LL (Social Semantic Web for Lifelong Learners)* format, starting from its needs analysis and learning framework sections.

2. How can self-regulation be scaffolded by a PLE?

Through an extensive study of the theoretical background of the personalisation of LLL and relevant research literature outcomes, implications and challenges of the concept of PLE have been discussed. Further, the smooth integration of formal and informal learning environments has been proposed, on the background of a student-centred framework for adult lifelong learners. To this end, several models for the detection of learning styles have been sieved through to choose the most effective to be applied in the scenario of this research.

3. How can adult lifelong learners' PLEs be characterised?

The exploration of the synergy of formal and informal learning in the dynamic construction of a lifelong learner's PLE has started the evaluation of added-value technological components among many available in the web-based learning landscape. A range of adaptive mechanisms and Social Semantic Web tools have been considered, as applications for providing implicit and explicit characterisation of adult lifelong learners' PLEs. As a result, the *SSW4LL* system has been built on Moodle 2.0 integrated with adaptation (conditional activities) and Semantic MediaWiki, Diigo and Google+ as Social Semantic Web tools.

The *SSW4LL* format has been implemented and evaluated with respect to its efficiency in supporting adult lifelong learners and making the characterisation of their PLEs easier for them.

Within this work, two general aims concerning all three parts of research exist. First, research conducted within this study aims at proposing concepts and approaches which are suitable for adult lifelong learners in general, rather than for one specific target within. However, the concepts and approaches are implemented and evaluated by addressing a cluster of novice learners in the course domain, but professionals in a specific field.

Secondly, since the objective of this research is to devise a format for the characterisation of adult lifelong learners' PLEs by combining the advantages of formal learning environments with those of informal learning environments, the resulting technological architecture should not lose its simplicity and should still be easy to use for teachers-facilitators.

Structure of the book

This book is organised in 4 chapters. The first chapter illustrates the current shift from formal to informal learning. An introduction of LLL is provided, describing definitions and main policies in Europe, and lifelong learners' characteristics, needs analysis and expectations. The third section of the chapter develops a sound analysis of the theoretical background of personalisation of lifelong learning: implications and challenges of the concept of PLE are discussed, as well as adaptive mechanisms and Social Semantic Web as tools for implicit and explicit personalisation of learning.

Chapter 2 starts the development of the characterisation of a PLE as a LLL tool by detailing the *SSW4LL* format. After an overview about the aims, possible scenarios and elements of the format, a motivated choice of adult lifelong learners' needs that *SSW4LL* aims to meet is developed. Subsequently, the chapter illustrates the learning paradigm and strategies that underpin the *SSW4LL* format. Then, the *SSW4LL* system, the technological architecture, is presented as a whole made up of components of formal and informal learning environments. The formal learning environment is devised by Moodle 2.0; a description and an evaluation of Moodle 2.0 features are provided, with a focus on the potential of its conditional activities as a suitable mechanism of learning adaptation. Concurrently, this part identifies the benefits of the Felder-Silverman learning style model, which was selected as the most suitable learning style model for the use in LMSs. The elements of the informal learning environment, Semantic MediaWiki, Diigo and Google+, are presented and their implications within the *SSW4LL* format are discussed. The next section of the chapter deals with the organisation of the format: the resources needed, a user case scenario and a flow chart of the steps of the format implementation are outlined. Finally, a SWOT analysis provides evaluation elements for the format.

Chapter 3 reports the case study *SSW4LL 2011*: its design and implementation steps and issues are detailed, and outcomes are discussed.

Chapter 4 concludes the study by highlighting its contributions and discussing limitations and future directions.

Ancona, Italy   Sabrina Leone

Acknowledgments

My very first thanks are addressed to Prof. Tommaso Leo for having been my supervisor and tenacious coach. I also thank all my PhD colleagues, in particular Giuliana and Carla for the many occasions of brainstorming, sharing and emotional support.

I also wish to express sincere thanks to all the international researchers and friends with whom I have been in touch, for their valuable support and advice during the development of the technological architecture of my research. By name, I'd like to thank Prof. Xiangen Hu, Dr. Stephan Downes, Prof. Kinshuk, Dr. Sabine Graf, Prof. Carla Limongelli, Dr. Vlad Posea, Dr. Scott Wilson, Dr. Kris Popat, Dr. Fridolin Wild, Dr. Alexander Mikroyannidis, Dr. Bernhard Hoisl, Dr. Lucas Anastasiou, Prof. Mary Cooch, Dr. Markus Krötzsch.

I would like to express special thanks to all the participants in *SSW4LL 2011*, for allowing me to complete my study.

A very special thank you goes to all my family, in particular to my parents, for having groomed me for my lifelong learning adventure; to Giovanni, for his endless and loving encouragement through the ups and downs during this work, and for his professional support during the implementation of my research; to my joyful and impatient Alessandro, for his caring hugs and smiles during the long weekends I spent to meet work deadlines.

Contents

Chapter 1
From Formal to Informal Learning: Scenario, Conditioning Elements and Evolutionary Steps

Abstract This chapter illustrates the current shift from formal to informal learning. The first section of the chapter provides an introduction to LLL, describing definitions and main policies in Europe, as first horizon in an international vision, with the aim of grounding the development of this research on updated official reports and on the orientation of macro-measures, to focus subsequently on a possible innovative learning format for adult lifelong learners.

The following outline of lifelong learners' characteristics, needs analysis, and expectations allow to profile the target learners of this study.

The third and final section of the chapter develops an extensive analysis of the theoretical background of personalisation of LLL: implications and challenges of the concept of PLE are discussed, as well as adaptive mechanisms and Social Semantic Web as tools for implicit and explicit personalisation of learning.

1.1 Lifelong Learning: Definitions and Main Policies in Europe

1.1.1 Lifelong Learning: Definitions and European Union Benchmarks

LLL is "a cultural term denoting a new paradigm. It is a shift away from the notion of provider-driven 'education' towards individualised learning" (UNESCO Institute for Education, 1999). It is "all learning activity undertaken throughout life, with the aim of improving knowledge, skills and competencies within a personal, civic, social and/or employment-related perspective" (European Commission, 2002).

Formal, non-formal and informal learning have become keywords of this age; in particular, there is an increasing understanding that learning occurs for the most part outside the traditional formal situations. Formal learning consists in the hierarchically structured, chronologically graded educational system running from primary through to tertiary institutions; non-formal learning takes place through

S. Leone, *Characterisation of a Personal Learning Environment as a Lifelong Learning Tool*, SpringerBriefs in Education, DOI 10.1007/978-1-4614-6274-3_1,

education organised for specific learners with specific learning objectives, outside the formal established system; informal learning allows persons to acquire attitudes, values, skills and knowledge from daily experience, within the individual's environment (such as family, friends, peer groups, the media and other influences) (UNESCO, 1999).

With the definition of the Lisbon objectives, the European Commission (EC) has posed a milestone in the evolution of learning (European Commission, 2001). The EC has highlighted the importance of LLL for all and the consequent need for change of traditional systems into more open and flexible systems, systems that could allow users to choose a learning path according to their learning needs and interests, at any time along their life (Leone, 2010).

EU member states are working to develop national LLL strategies for all learning spheres (formal, non-formal and informal), for all levels of education (pre-school, primary, secondary, tertiary and adult education) and for all the learning activities that individuals take up along their life (European Commission, 2008b).

In May 2009 the Council agreed Education and Training 2020 (ET 2020) (European Commission, 2009), an updated strategic framework for European cooperation in education and training as a prosecution of the Lisbon strategy (European Commission, 2011a).

In 2003 the European Council had adopted five benchmarks (Table 1.1), to be achieved by 2010, to guide policy making and to monitor progress, both at the EU and national levels, towards commonly agreed strategic objectives for education and training. By ET 2020 the Council adopted a renewed set of benchmarks, to be achieved by 2020, that are characterised by new benchmarks on early childhood education and on tertiary attainment among the young adult population; a broadening of the benchmark on low reading achievement to cover mathematics and science; a reduction for the benchmark for early school leaving and an increase in the target level for adult participation in LLL. The 2010 benchmark on increasing the completion rate of upper secondary education has been discontinued on the basis that it is closely linked to the maintained benchmark on early school leaving.

Furthermore, two of these five benchmarks—to reduce the number of early school leavers and to increase the share of young adults holding tertiary education qualifications (in bold in Table 1.1)—have been given further importance having been selected as headline targets for the Europe 2020 for socio-economic development in 2020.

Broadly, there has been progress over the period since 2000. However, only one benchmark has been met. Adult participation in LLL progressed reasonably well until 2005, but has stagnated since then (Fig. 1.1).

LLL had many breaks in the time series, which tend to overstate the progress made, especially in 2003. Therefore, the 2002–2003 line on adult LLL participation is dotted.

Countries in the upper right quadrant have performance above the level of the EU benchmark (high share of adults participating in LLL) and have been successful in increasing this share further in the past, while countries in the lower left quadrant have below EU benchmark performance and have not been successful in increasing this share in the past.

Table 1.1 EU benchmarks sets for 2010 and 2020

EU benchmarks for 2010	EU benchmarks for 2020
1 No more than 10 % early school leavers	At least 95 % of children between 4 years old and the age for starting compulsory primary education should participate in early childhood education
2 Decrease of at least 20 % in the percentage of low-achieving pupils in reading literacy	**The share of early leavers from education and training should be less than 10 %**
3 At least 85 % of young people should have completed upper secondary education	The share of low-achieving 15-years olds in reading, mathematics and science should be less than 15%
4 Increase of at least 15 % in the number of tertiary graduates in Mathematics, Science and Technology (MST), with a simultaneous decrease in the gender imbalance	**The share of 30–34 year olds with tertiary educational attainment should be at least 40 %**
5 12.5 % of the adult population should participate in lifelong learning	An average of at least 15 % of adults should participate in lifelong learning

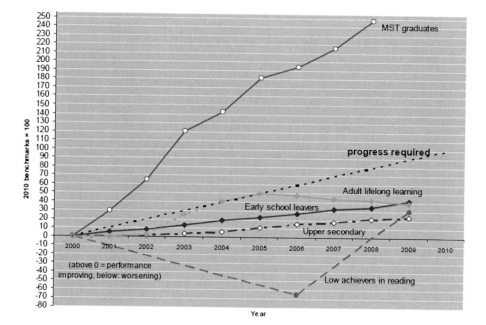

Fig. 1.1 Progress towards meeting the five benchmarks for 2010 (2000–2009). *Source*: European Commission DG EAC (European Commission, 2011a). *Note*: On the *y*-axis the value 100 represents the achievement of EU 2010 benchmarks

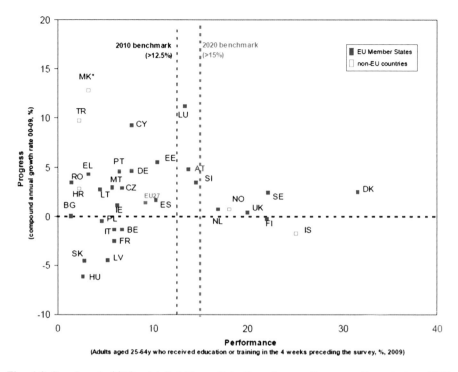

Fig. 1.2 Benchmark 2010—Adult LLL participation. *Source*: European Commission, JRC/ CRELL calculations based on LFS data (European Commission, 2011a). Notes: *MK*: The former Yugoslav Republic of Macedonia. The *y*-axis shows the percentage of annual growth in the period 2000–2009

Increasing the participation by adults in LLL is a highly important EU policy objective. Figure 1.2 shows that the EU as a whole has now reached a participation rate of 9.3 %, against the 2010 benchmark of 12.5 %. In detail, many EU countries showed a sound improvement in their performance in the first half of the decade, and a slight decline since 2005. Best performers are Denmark, Sweden, Finland, Iceland and the UK, with a participation rate of over 20 %. Bulgaria, Romania and Greece show the lowest participation rates, but improving performance. On the other hand Hungary and especially Slovakia perform well below the benchmark level, with a declining trend (European Commission, 2011a).

A major element of the LLL process is informal learning. The results of the EU survey on adult education (AES) (European Commission, 2011a) highlight that in 2007, the EU participation rate for informal learning among adults was 46.5 %, notably higher than the rate for non-formal activities (32.7 %) and formal education (6.3 %).

The most used learning resources are printed materials (used by 35 % of learners) and computers (27 %). The exchange of knowledge between members of the family, friends or colleagues is indicated by almost one-fifth of the adults interviewed. The least frequent way of learning is visiting learning centres or libraries (Fig. 1.3).

	Total	Learn from a family member. friend or colleague	Learn using printed materials	Learn using computers	Learn through television/ radio/ video	Learn by guided tours of museums. historical/natural/ industrial sites	Learn visiting learning centres (including libraries)
EU 22 countries	46.5	19.2	35	26.9	18.3	10.4	8.1
Belgium	34.9	15.2	22.5	24.3	7.1	4.8	7.4
Bulgaria	28.0	8.6	18.3	17.3	13.1	2.0	3.2
Czech Republic	54.7	18.9	42.1	33.2	29.0	8.5	6.5
Germany	52.4	18.8	40.4	33.9	15.8	8.0	6.8
Estonia	44.8	27.2	28.9	27.0	22.6	15.9	14.4
Greece	20.7	5.6	16.3	11.8	8.3	2.0	2.4
Spain	28.0	11.1	16.6	15.7	6.7	5.2	5.1
France	63.8	26.5	46.1	42.1	39.8	24.6	17.1
Italy	41.2	24	26.6	23.0	15.1	13.3	4.6
Cyprus	63.6	33.3	44.7	22.8	32.7	8.7	5.1
Latvia	53.9	33.1	41.3	28.3	36.8	10.5	11.3
Lithuania	45.3	20.7	32.7	23.9	16.4	3.9	9.6
Hungary	26.2	11.6	18.6	15.2	16.4	6.2	5.7
Netherlands	:	:	:	:	:	:	:
Austria	75.7	44.1	61.7	43.1	38.4	31.5	14.4
Poland	25.4	9	20.5	17.1	11.3	3.2	6.4
Portugal	38.9	24.4	22.2	20.5	10.1	5.3	3.4
Slovenia	62.0	26.8	45.8	41.7	26.7	20	26.1
Slovakia	84.1	38.5	67.6	51.5	69.8	19.7	20.5
Finland	54.6	17.3	38.3	32.1	12.1	11.0	27.8
Sweden	76.0	43.9	60.2	54.9	25.4	22.6	23.5
United Kingdom	53.7	14.3	50.4	19.0	13.0	3.3	5.7
Croatia	44.6	24.8	30.1	27.1	25.4	8.0	9.8
Norway	72.3	45.5	51.6	47.5	26.6	19.7	18.1

Fig. 1.3 Participation in informal learning by learning method (25–64 years old, 2007 rates). *Source*: Eurostat (AES) (European Commission, 2011a). *Note*: Data for Poland are not included in the EU average because of the very high non-response rate. High values for Slovakia might be due to the likelihood that random learning was considered as informal learning

The survey results point to relevant disparities in participation in adult LLL activities related to socio-economic factors (those who take less advantage of these opportunities are older people, the less educated and the non-employed). This is also the case for informal activities. The highest participation rates are those for adults between 25 and 34 years old (51.4 %) (Fig. 1.4). The next age group (35–54) is not so far behind, while a notable decrease in the participation rate is found after 55, as it drops to 38.4 %. The decrease is around one-half in some countries, such as Greece, Hungary and Portugal, whereas it is around 10 % in certain Nordic and Baltic countries, Slovakia and Austria.

Disparities are generally much larger in respect to highest educational level attained (Fig. 1.5). The highly educated are 2.4 times more likely to participate in informal learning: their participation rate is 66.6 % against just 28 % for adults with at most lower secondary. Such disparities are lowest in Norway, Sweden, Slovakia and Austria, which also had less extreme differences among age groups. The gap is much larger in some eastern and southern countries, such as Bulgaria, Greece, Hungary and Poland, where the most educated are 4.5–7 times more likely to participate in informal learning.

Particular ways of learning are more often utilised by low-educated adults, namely learning from family members, friends or colleagues and learning through television/radio/video. Computers and learning centres are apparently more difficult to access, and particularly the latter are mainly used by adults with tertiary education.

	Total	25-34	35-54	55-64
EU 22 countries	46.5	51.4	47.6	38.4
Belgium	34.9	42.4	36.5	25.3
Bulgaria	28.0	34.8	28.9	18.6
Czech Republic	54.7	59.4	55.9	47.7
Germany	52.4	53.8	54.3	45.7
Estonia	44.8	48.5	44.7	40.3
Greece	20.7	24.6	22.3	11.7
Spain	28.0	33.0	27.9	20.3
France	63.8	72.9	63.1	54.4
Italy	41.2	49.6	42.6	29.5
Cyprus	63.6	71.3	62.3	55.7
Latvia	53.9	55.8	54.0	51.5
Lithuania	45.3	53.4	46.5	30.9
Hungary	26.2	33.7	27.1	17.4
Netherlands	:	:	:	:
Austria	75.7	77.1	77.6	68.8
Poland	25.4	31.3	25.3	17.1
Portugal	38.9	50.6	38.0	25.8
Slovenia	62.0	72.1	62.1	50.1
Slovakia	84.1	87.6	83.7	79.9
Finland	54.6	61.0	55.1	47.8
Sweden	76.0	80.7	76.4	71.1
United Kingdom	53.7	56.3	55.8	46.1
Croatia	44.6	53.4	44.1	35.4
Norway	72.3	74.0	73.8	67.1

Fig. 1.4 Participation in informal learning by age (2007 rates). *Source*: Eurostat (AES) (European Commission, 2011a). *Note*: Data for Poland are not included in the EU average because of the very high non-response rate

In reference to the labour market status, informal learning is more frequent among employed (51.1 %) than unemployed (41.6 %) or inactive adults (34 %).

Figure 1.6 shows Italy results against EU 2010 benchmarks. In particular, Italian adult participation in LLL was 6 % in 2009, far below the EU 9.3 % and the 2010 benchmark of 12.5 %.

1.1.2 European Policy Progress and Future Prospects

The scenario illustrated in the previous section, on the basis of a EC report (2011a), and a recent Cedefop (2011) working paper about lifelong guidance across Europe, empha-sises that during 2007–2010 throughout the EU Member States the progress made is evident in promoting systemic sustainability, new reforms, improved coordination

	Total	Highest education level attained			Labour market status		
		Lower secondary	Upper secondary	Tertiary education	Employed	Unemployed	Inactive
EU 22 countries	46.5	28.0	49.3	66.6	51.1	41.6	34.0
Belgium	34.9	17.1	34.0	53.5	40.2	27.0	22.0
Bulgaria	28.0	10.1	24.6	54.9	33.6	15.3	16.5
Czech Republic	54.7	32.0	53.7	79.0	58.2	45.6	44.7
Germany	52.4	31.7	49.0	75.2	54.9	46.2	46.5
Estonia	44.8	29.9	40.4	57.5	47.2	25.5	37.8
Greece	20.7	9.2	20.6	41.0	24.1	21.6	10.8
Spain	28.0	18.3	31.2	42.2	30.4	26.2	20.6
France	63.8	44.7	65.8	85.3	68.5	59.8	49.2
Italy	41.2	26.3	51.2	67.9	47.5	38.8	28.1
Cyprus	63.6	50.8	63.8	75.4	64.9	55.9	60.2
Latvia	53.9	36.9	52.4	67.5	58.1	29.6	47.8
Lithuania	45.3	18.7	38.3	69.4	51.7	35.6	26.9
Hungary	26.2	10.2	24.5	55.4	33.6	14.1	13.8
Netherlands	:	:	:	:	:	:	:
Austria	75.7	60.7	76.6	89.5	78.9	67.0	68.1
Poland	25.4	7.7	20.3	55.5	31.0	19.5	13.9
Portugal	38.9	29.7	55.8	71.2	42.3	41.5	25.0
Slovenia	62.0	38.0	61.5	83.0	66.4	57.7	48.7
Slovakia	84.1	71.3	82.3	93.3	86.5	75.5	77.0
Finland	54.6	41.8	51.4	67.5	57.3	47.2	47.0
Sweden	76.0	60.8	76.9	87.5	78.1	66.2	69.8
United Kingdom	53.7	30.3	55.0	76.1	61.2	44.4	32.6
Croatia	44.6	23.2	47.5	76.6	52.7	36.8	31.4
Norway	72.3	60.1	70.0	85.7	75.5	63.0	59.2

Fig. 1.5 Participation in informal learning by educational attainment and labour status (2007 rates). *Source*: Eurostat (AES) (European Commission, 2011a). *Note*: Data for Poland are not included in the EU average because of the very high non-response rate

ITALY

	Italy		EU average		EU Benchmarks	
	2000	2009	2000	2009	2010	2020
Participation in early childhood education (4 years old - year before start of comp. primary)	100%	98.8%[08]	85.6%	92.3%[08]		95%
Low achievers (15 year-olds; PISA study results) — Reading	18.9%	21.0%	21.3%	20.0%	17.0 %	15%
Low achievers (15 year-olds; PISA study results) — Mathematics	32.8%[06]	24.9%	24.0%[06]	22.2%	-	15%
Low achievers (15 year-olds; PISA study results) — Science	25.3%[06]	20.6%	20.3%[06]	17.7%	-	15%
Early leavers from education and training (age 18-24)	25.1%	19.2%	17.6%	14.4%	10 %	10%
Upper secondary attainment (age 20-24)	69.4%	76.3%	76.6%	78.6%	85 %	-
MST graduates (higher education) — Increase since 2000	-	62.9%[08]	-	37.2%[08]	+15 %	-
MST graduates (higher education) — Share of females	36.6%	38.4%[08]	30.7%	32.6%[08]	Improve gender balance	-
Higher education attainment (age 30-34)	11.6%	19.0%	22.4%	32.3%	-	40%
Adult participation in lifelong learning (age 25-64; 4 weeks period)	6.3 %[04]	6.0 %	8.5%[03]	9.3% p	12.5 %	15%
Investment in education Public spending on education,% of GDP	4.55%	4.29%[07]	4.88%	4.96%[07]	-	-

Fig. 1.6 Italy results against EU 2010 benchmarks. *Source*: Eurostat (UOE, LFS) and OECD (PISA) (European Commission, 2011a). 03 = 2003, 06 = 2006, 07 =2007, 08 =2008; *p* provisional. PISA: reading: 18 EU countries; maths and science: 25 EU countries. "EU Benchmarks" are defined as "EU average performance levels" (weighted averages)

mechanisms and more cohesive and cooperative guidance[1] communities. Nevertheless, further development is necessary. Instruments and cooperation mechanisms are needed to increase participation in LLL, to have individuals' informal and non-formal learning validated, to support transparency of qualifications between institutions, systems and countries, and to consequently ensure smooth mobility of learners and workers in the European labour market.

In the meantime, the EC has been developing the European qualifications framework (EQF) for LLL (European Parliament and Council of the European Union, 2008) and the European credit system for vocational education and training (ECVET) (Cedefop, 2011; European Parliament and Council of the European Union, 2009).

Further, in March 2010, with the Budapest–Vienna Ministerial Declaration, the European higher education area (EHEA) finally became a reality.[2] This Declaration, while supporting the consolidation of the EHEA during 2011–2020, aims at implementing guidance-related objectives in tertiary education to complete the reforms underway (mobility, enhancement of graduate employability and quality higher education for all) and to foster high quality, flexible and student-centred learning as a way of empowering the individual in all forms of education.

Parallel to the above, the Council conclusions (Council of European Union, 2010) emphasise measures targeted at providing individualised support (guidance, mentoring and skills training) particularly during the early stages of a university course to improve graduation rates for students, specifically for disadvantaged learners.

One key dimension in the future work is to find innovative and synergetic ways to reinforce policy-strategy planning and implementation between national, regional and local levels, and to activate greater collective strategic initiative between the relevant sectors (education, training and employment) and key operators (including social partners, employers, guidance practitioners, guidance service users). Finally, recent EU level policies have addressed the need to improve LLL and career management opportunities by simultaneously developing a coherent and holistic lifelong guidance provision to help learners make well-informed choices and decisions on their participation in education, training and working.

---

[1] Guidance as referring to a continuous process that enables citizens at any age and at any point in their lives to identify their capacities, competences and interests, to make educational, training and occupational decisions and to manage their individual life paths in learning, work and other settings in which those capacities and competences are learned and/or used. Guidance covers a range of individual and collective activities relating to information-giving, counselling, competence assessment, support and the teaching of decision-making and career management skills (CEDEFOP, 2011, p. 18). The Council of the EU adopted two guidance resolutions on strengthening policies, systems and practices in guidance throughout life in Europe (Council of the European Union, 2004) and on better integrating lifelong guidance into LLL strategies (Council of the European Union, 2008). Also the FEDORA (2007) highlights the value of guidance provision and seeks the support of all stakeholders. FEDORA (http://www.fedora.eu.org) is a European Association whose members work as guidance practitioners in a variety of roles in higher education institutions.

[2] The Bologna process (started in 1999) establishes the framework for cooperation with 46 countries to create an EHEA that ensures more comparable, compatible and coherent systems of higher education in Europe.

In this view, the challenge for adult education consists first of all in the delivery of a service that meets adequately the adult learner's needs and the requirements of labour market and society. Secondly, adult education should stimulate the demand further. To this end, an effective and efficient adult education system includes strongly interrelated key elements as the policies, the structures of governance and the systems of education (European Commission, 2007).

Within these macro-areas, the following measures could allow to overcome obstacles due to the multidimensional character of participation:

- develop a greater proximity between learning and learner in terms of place and offer diversified opportunities of learning that meet individuals' specific needs (i.e. in e-learning);
- allow a flexible access to assessment, validation and acknowledgement of learning outcomes, and consequently to certification and qualification;
- extend access to higher education, offer financial support according to the demand and motivate full-time or part-time learning;
- encourage individuals to invest on learning for both personal fulfilment and better occupability.

In this scenario, e-learning, if supported by a suitable pedagogic paradigm, becomes an added-value learning mode and tool thanks to the flexibility that it offers in terms of time and space (*anytime, anywhere*), of personalisation of paths, of increase in interaction, of tracking of the progress in individual competences and knowledge (Leone, 2010). Research highlights that success key of technology-enhanced learning is a learner-centred approach (Alberici, Catarsi, Colapietro, & Loiodice, 2007; Varisco, 2002), that is a constructivist approach (Barr & Tagg, 1995; Jonassen & Land, 2000; Von Glasersfeld, 1998) which is attentive to emotional/relational aspects (Calvani, 2006; Kern, Ware, & Warschauer, 2004; Kort & Reilly, 2002).

This overview on macro-policies for LLL allows to draw a line to micro-level expected contributions. With particular reference to the aims of this research, the preceding analysis signals the need for more personal, social and participatory approaches that support learners in becoming active users and co-producers of learning resources, rather in gaining control over the learning process as a whole, and in pursuing personal life goals and needs. In particular, there is an increasing understanding that learning occurs for the most part outside the traditional formal situations, especially for adult lifelong learners.

1.2 The Lifelong Learner: Characteristics, Needs Analysis and Expectations

European policies for the achievement of the Lisbon and the ET 2020 objectives have focussed on the individual as the activator of economical, cultural and social growth of our society and of the systems within.

In a LLL vision, the individual, the "active citizen", becomes a primary resource of knowledge. The individual's empowerment extends little by little to his/her context and to society as in a network. Through this process old and new borders of knowledge, competence and skills merge and widen, and they are filtered by the key skill of "learning to learn" and of acquiring knowledge and know-how which can be exploited in various contexts.

1.2.1　Lifelong Learners' Features

Lifelong learners, who must be equipped to direct their own learning and development (especially following their formal schooling), are characterised as demonstrating perseverance, initiative and adaptive abilities. Lifelong learners are self-regulated learners (Leone, 2010). Self-regulation relates to an ability to recognise a need for further learning as well as to be proactive in gaining access to and accomplishing learning (Martinez-Pons, 2002; Zimmerman, 2002).

The plans of the EU on LLL (EAEA, 2006; European Commission, 2000, 2006, 2007) let outline the distinctive elements common to the persons constantly engaged in improving as professionals and as individuals. Lifelong learners:

- have a novice's approach, rather than an expert's attitude, that let them take advantage of all learning opportunities;
- relate and exploit the knowledge and the competences they have acquired in other contexts;
- are flexible and adaptable to favour learning;
- are always fond of learning something for the pleasure of acquiring and for personal empowerment;
- are curious and feed their curiosity;
- learn in many ways, both formal and informal settings and by different learning strategies for different situations;
- teach others to improve their competence.

The predominance of some of these features characterise the following lifelong learners' profiles (Table 1.2) (Leone, 2010).

1.2.2　Lifelong Learners' Needs Analysis and Expectations

The European reference framework of key competences for LLL (European Parliament and Council of the European Union, 2006) sustains that each citizen needs a wide range of key competences[3] for adapting flexibly to a rapidly changing world.

---

[3]The Reference Framework sets out eight key competences (1) Communication in the mother tongue; (2) Communication in foreign languages; (3) Mathematical competence and basic competences in science and technology; (4) Digital competence; (5) Learning to learn; (6) Social and civic competences; (7) Sense of initiative and entrepreneurship and (8) Cultural awareness and expression. The eight key competences are defined as a combination of knowledge, skills and attitudes appropriate to the context, and they contain several themes such as critical thinking, creativity, initiative, problem solving, risk assessment, decision taking and constructive management of feelings.

Table 1.2 Lifelong learners' profiles

Lifelong learner's profiles	Definition	Elements The lifelong learner…
Active	Student's active participation in the learning process through involvement, engagement, reflection and academic skills as analysis, synthesis and evaluation (Bloom's taxonomy).	✓ Identifies personal objectives and the necessary steps to achieve them. ✓ Uses resources (human resources and tools) to achieve objectives. ✓ Learns to solve any kind of problem (problem-solving approach). ✓ Uses time well (time management).
Cooperative	Student's way of dealing with people and contributing to group works: sharing of leadership and responsibility and consensus building through cooperation.	✓ Is a leader who can guide and support others. ✓ Constantly seeks, identifies and creates effective contacts with others. ✓ Enjoys working in group towards a common goal.
Creative	Creative thinking, i.e. the production of something new or original, in order to stimulate curiosity and promote divergence through flexibility, originality, competence, elaboration, brainstorming, modification, visualisation, associative thinking, metaphorical thinking.	✓ Generates a large number of unusual ideas or solutions to problems. ✓ Is enterprising. ✓ Is imaginative and innovative. ✓ Sees difficulties as opportunities and challenges as interesting.
Critical	Critical thinking, i.e. the intellectually disciplined process of conceptualisation, application, analysis, synthesis and/or evaluation of information gathered by observation, experience, reflection, reasoning or communication, as a guide to belief and action.	✓ Examines situations from different points of view before coming to conclusions. ✓ Separates facts from opinions. ✓ Appreciates and tries to understand others' thoughts, emotions and behaviours.
Strategic	Construction of personal meanings and awareness of personal thinking. Development of the ability to analyse, reflect on and understand personal cognitive and learning process—meta-cognition.	✓ Plans how to face learning situations satisfactorily. ✓ Practises, monitors and evaluates consciously what he/she is taught. ✓ Develops and uses a series techniques and tactics.
Autonomous	More control on one's own learning. This implies self-government abilities at various degrees.	✓ Shows responsibility and initiative in the development of his/her learning agenda. ✓ Reflects on what has learnt, evaluate effects, develops and uses self-assessment criteria. ✓ Self-regulates his/her interaction with others and the appropriate use of resources.

Education plays an important role in ensuring that citizens acquire these key competences that enable them for further learning and working throughout their life. "Learning to learn", one of the eight key competences, particularly outlines the importance of guidance in acquiring and processing new knowledge and skills as well as seeking support for pursuing one's learning and career goals. Above all, at-risk groups should be supported in the acquisition of these key competences, including people with low basic and low literacy skills, early school leavers, the long-term unemployed and those returning to work after a period of extended leave, older people, migrants and people with disabilities (Cedefop, 2011).

At a European level, the following progress has been made to sustain citizens' empowerment: launching the concept of LLL; adopting eight key competences for LLL; establishing the European Qualifications Framework for LLL (EQF) and the European Credit System for Vocational Education and Training (ECVET); publishing the European guidelines on the validation of informal and non-formal learning; acknowledging the value of learning outcomes (Cedefop, 2011).

Anyhow, improvements in the delivery of adult learning are essential to raise participation and ensure quality learning outcomes (European Commission, 2006, 2011b). Quality assurance, in particular, is crucial within the EU reforms in education and training. "Quality of provision is affected by policy, resources, accommodation and a host of other factors, but the key factor is the quality of the staff involved in delivery. They have to be able to address the different needs of the specific groups" (European Commission, 2011b, p. 26).

In this regard, the ALPINE study (European Commission, 2008a) identified a number of key characteristics of the adult education and training sector staff, across Europe.

The sector is varied. Providers differ in size, the kind of learning they offer, the way they are funded and managed, their target groups and the learning methods used. Staff within the sector has different employment conditions (from permanent, fulltime contracts to more precarious, freelance contracts). They have a variety of backgrounds, are well educated but with little profession-related training, and tend to join the profession later in life after gaining work experience elsewhere. Volunteering is also common in some countries.

This means that the provision of training to personnel within the sector needs to be particularly flexible, with more emphasis on continuing professional development through short courses, work-based learning and induction programmes than on initial training. Generally, the professions of teaching or training in adult learning are poorly regulated.

As follow-on from the ALPINE study, the EC undertook a study on key competences for adult learning professionals (Broek & Buiskool, 2010). The study provided elements of a competence profile for adult learning professionals, that is a starting point for further peer learning and a contribution to meeting the need underlined in ET 2020 "to ensure high quality teaching, to provide adequate initial teacher education, continuous professional development for teachers and trainers and to make teaching an attractive career choice" (European Commission, 2011b, p. 28).

As a result, the ALPINE study takes into account the wide range of activities that are being carried out in the adult learning sector by the different staff in different

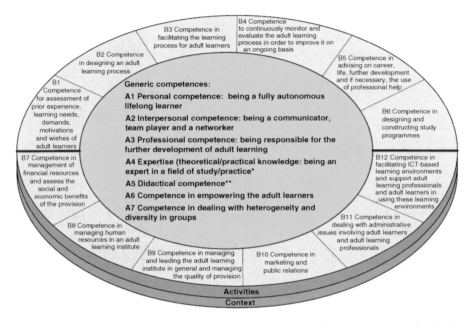

Fig. 1.7 Graphic representation of the set of key competences of adult learning professionals (Broek & Buiskool, 2010). *Single asterisk*: For professionals not directly involved in the learning process, the expertise concerns not subject knowledge, but specific (e.g. managerial, administrative or ICT) expertise. *Double asterisks*: For professionals not directly involved in the learning process or supportive in a managerial, administrative way; the didactical competence is less relevant

contexts in the field of adult learning. The outcome of this analysis is a set of key competences (Fig. 1.7).

Since competences are required to accomplish an activity in a specific context, the following graphic representation shows three layers (1) competences, (2) activities (containing a list of activities adult learning professionals are carrying out) and (3) context (containing variables that determine the context in which activities need to be carried out).

Competences are distinguished in generic competences, (i.e. those that every adult learning professional ought to possess) and specific competences (i.e. that are needed for professionals responsible for a specific field of activity, as facilitating learning, managing the institute, etc.).

Thirteen fields of activity have been identified; not all activities need to be carried out by one professional, but can be divided amongst a group of professionals (e.g. managers, teachers or support staff).

The context in which adult education is provided affects the exact shaping of the competences and the weight they receive. The context depends on variables like the target groups, the team composition, the education programmes delivered in the institute, the attention to professional development, the exact mission of the institute and so on.

The identified competences may serve as a base, or rather a frame of reference for improvement or change of existing adult learning practices in a variety of ways.

In this respect it is also important to mention that not all policy implications apply equally to all countries included in this study. In some cases policy directions are already in place, while for others there may be less relevance due to different learning cultures, government structures or regulations.

1.3   Personalising Lifelong Learning: Approaches, Methodologies and Tools

The current focus of the EU policies and of research literature on LLL and on the individual as the activator of economical, cultural and social growth of our society implies the need for a common understanding on the concepts of personalising learning, personalised learning and PLE.

Further, numerous and multifaceted theoretical backgrounds have underpinned the ongoing merging of formal and informal learning.

The following paragraphs aim to provide a literature review about the personalisation of learning, dedicating particular attention to the shift from organisation-centred to learner-centred learning environments, to the different extensions of the concept of PLE and to the latest tools of implicit and explicit personalisation of technology-enhanced learning.

1.3.1   Personalising Learning: A Common Understanding

Personalised learning has been defined with different emphasis by many authors over time. Both in the past and in recent times, a basic common view is that each learner should be able to choose a tailored learning path, in order to meet personal needs, interests and abilities (Bentley & Miller, 2004); to promote both independence and dependability (Downes, 2007; Siemens, 2004); to enhance social skills and sense of responsibility toward others (Keller, 1968; Parkhurst, 1922); to improve creative, intellectual, social and moral growth and develop personality fully (Claparède, 1920; Fullan, 2009; OECD, 2006).

The Dalton Plan (nineteenth century), the Winnetka Plan (begin of twentieth century), the Project Method (early twentieth century), the Mastery learning (1950s–1960s) and the Personalized System of Instruction (1960s) were developed on this background, with particular accent of the last four on programmed instruction (Washburne, 1941), problem solving and teacher as a facilitator (Kilpatrick, 1918), instructional design (Bloom, 1985) and peer learning (Keller, 1968), respectively. In the 1980s the Theory of Multiple Intelligences (Gardner, 1983), as opposed to a general intelligence factor among correlated abilities, highlighted that not only do human beings have many different ways to learn and process information, but that these are independent of each other. In the same period, within the humanistic approach to psychology, Person-Centred Teaching and Learning theory (Rogers, 1983) was elaborated as a totally new approach to education, for learners of all age groups independent of their social background.

More recently, Hargreaves (2004) has referred to *personalising learning* rather than *personalised learning*, in order to emphasise that it should be more of a process than a product. Hargreaves has established nine gateways to personalised learning: student voice; assessment for learning; learning to learn; new technologies; curriculum; advice and guidance; mentoring and coaching; workforce development and school design and organisation.

Personalising learning is the process which empowers the learner to decide what, where, when and how to learn (National College, 2011), and to promote personal development through self-realisation, self-enhancement and self-development. The learner should be seen as active, responsible and self-motivated, a co-author of the script that determines how education is delivered (Leadbeater, 2004), often with extensive use of technology in the process. Personalised learning is a means of renewing inclusiveness, increasing student participation and providing direction in the development of twenty-first century education. The rationale for personalised learning is to meet learner's needs, goals and preferences in order to ensure that every student achieves the highest standard possible. The emphasis in relation to personalising education is that learning is lifelong and, therefore, reaching beyond the traditional confines of schools: people do not learn for the school, but for life (OECD, 2006).

Personalisation is thus a strategy aimed at designing and implementing learner-centred institutional practices and support mechanisms (Ewing, 2007; Garcìa Hoz, 1981; Maharey, 2007), and at drawing on wider resources for learning beyond formal education, by creating new flexibilities to meet new demands (Bentley, 2005).

Personalised learning becomes possible when individuals are capable of identifying their needs, and suppliers are capable of recognising, helping elicit and responding in customised ways to the distinctiveness of an individual's needs (Bentley & Miller, 2004). Consequently, education systems are to be reorganised to start with the student (Hopkins, 2007), to be less concerned with what knowledge is acquired and more interested in how knowledge is used. The priority is to know students well enough to make every learning experience motivating the students to learn more and lifelong (Littky & Allen, 1999).

The concept of personalised learning is most commonly associated in the USA with differentiated instruction (Fullan, 2009). Personalisation may differ from differentiation in that it affords the learner a degree of choice about what is learned, when it is learned and how it is learned, according to personal targets, learning styles and multiple intelligences.

From a research perspective, the concept of individualised learning[4] is not synonymous with personalised learning, either. The former defines a teacher-driven

---

[4]Individualised learning was developed in the 1970s as an alternative approach to traditional group instructional approaches. At this time individualised learning allowed students to have more time and appropriate instruction if they needed it. The curriculum content and work undertaken by students was set and assessed by the classroom teacher.

approach to learning aiming to guarantee all students the achievement of the same learning objectives. Students usually work independently on the materials pre-scribed for them, depending on their demonstrated level of competence, different rhythms, times, learning style and needs (Joyce, Weil, & Calhoun, 2000). On the other hand, personalisation aims to valorise the learner's full potential and to empower individuals through knowledge sharing and co-construction. The learner, guided by the teacher, is an active co-designer of the learning pathway experience (Maharey, 2007).

The partners of the European Grundtvig Project LEADLAB (2010) propose a shared European definition of the term personalisation based on an andragogic con-cept of education (Knowles, 1970) within the context of the Non Vocational Adult Education (NVAE) and on the European experiences of personalisation in adult edu-cation. This definition includes the following recurrent features: full involvement of the learner (cognitive, social, emotional); empowerment of awareness of the learning process; development of self-regulation and self-assessment of learning; learning path, rather than instructional curriculum or training programme; co-design of the learning path; learning challenges instead of learning objectives; achievable results.

Nowadays, *anytime–anywhere* learning has become the label of globalised edu-cation, where time and space are experienced as compressed and filled thanks to information and communication technologies (ICTs).

ICTs can be a powerful tool for personalised learning, as they allow learners access research and information, and communicate, debate, participate. In the rheto-ric around twenty-first century skills, personalised learning is often equated with "customisation" (as found in the business world), with digital personalisation used to frame the learning experience as highly efficient, with little consideration for a suitable and necessary learning approach.

Finally, Campbell, Robinson, Neelands, Hewston, & Mazzoli (2007) draw upon Leadbeater's model of surface and deep personalisation (Leadbeater, 2004, 2009), where the student steadily progresses from consumer to producer behaviour. This view calls attention to a great deal of crossover with PLEs, particularly in relation to user-generated content and sharing within a community of practice (Wheeler, 2011b).

1.3.2 PLE and Related Concepts

Since its appearance, the concept of PLE has challenged the existing education systems and institutions. New forms of learning are based on trying things and action, rather than on more abstract knowledge.

According to the PLE approach, the learner is able to manage his/her own knowl-edge by managing connections (Leo, Manganello, & Chen, 2010). In this view, the PLE offers a portal to the world, through which learners can explore and create, fol-lowing their own interests and directions, interacting at all times with their friends and community (Attwell, 2008). The PLE is a learner-centred environment, whose shape and content can be personalised by the learner throughout his/her LLL activities

(Leo et al., 2010; Lubesky, 2006). The PLE is a technological tool, but, at the same time, it is the result of the individual's interaction within a community of different services. The PLE favours the creation of a different kind of knowledge: knowledge in the Virtual Learning Environment (VLE) is static, declarative and authority-based; knowledge in the PLE, instead, is dynamic, tacit/non-declarative, non-explicit, constructed by the people who are working inside the PLE. In this way, learning comes through learners' participation on a community (Downes, 2010).

Different PLEs are connected through with an application. Typically, people learning in this way refer to as "learning through social networks". However, personal knowledge consists of neural connections, rather than social connections. Social connections are part of a Personal Learning Network (PLN) (Via, 2010), and a learner uses his/her PLN in order to create a Personal Neural Network (PNN) (Downes, 2010). Consequently, learning turns from accusation of facts and data into creation of a new set of neural connections in the mind.

This is the difference between learning in a PLE and learning in a traditional manner. It is the difference between simple and complex: simple is learning a fact; complex is learning a fact in the context of a network and learning not only the fact but all the associated information around that fact.

Learning is a total state, and not a collection of specific states. For this reason, learning is obtained through immersion in an environment, rather than through acquisition of particular entities; it's expressed functionally (personal capacities) rather than cognitively (bits of knowledge).

A degree of overlap exists between the terms PLE and PLN. PLE has received greater adoption in higher education, while PLN seems to be more prominent among K-12 (primary/secondary) educators. Anyhow, they differ. A PLE is more of a concept than a particular toolset: it can be defined as a distributed, personal, open, learner-autonomy environment. These conceptual attributes influence the types of tools individuals select to engage in learning. Often, PLEs are presented in contrast to organisational LMSs. On the other hand, a PLN is a structure that reflects relatedness to other people. Information sources (i.e. Google or databases) can be part of a PLN. A PLN is grown by adding new people or connections, and it is a reflection of social and information networks (and analysis methods) (Downes, 2010).

Motschnig-Pitrik and Mallich (2004) refer to PLE as Person-Centred e-Learning (PCeL). Karrer (2008) considers the term PLE as a limited expression to indicate what actually is a Personal Work and Learning Environment (PWLE), that is the set of methods, skills and tools to perform day-to-day knowledge work activities, and where the user acquires information and knowledge. In Karrer's view, the concept of Personal Knowledge Environment (PKE) is better than PLE, but, still, the author sustains that it sounds passive (a PKE is where knowledge is stored), as opposed to PWLE, that is where the user acts more actively, by working and learning. All of the requirements that are foreseen for a PWLE apply equally well to a Personal Learning Environment Framework (PLEF) (Chatti, Agustiawan, Jarke, & Specht, 2010), even though the authors believe that learning and knowledge work are two sides of the same coin and thus can be used interchangeably, rather than simultaneously in a same term. PLEF's primary aim is to help learners create custom learning mash-ups using a wide variety of digital media and data. A PLEF includes: personalisation, social features, social filtering, various Web 2.0 concepts and technologies (mash-ups, widgets, aggregation, OpenID, RSS, etc.), flexibility and extensibility, Web browser platform, ease of use.

Pettenati (2010) adopts Personal Knowledge Environment (PKE) as an extension of the notion of PLE to highlight the multiple dimensions of such a complex-system concept. A PKE is a technology-enhanced window mediating higher education and lifelong knowledge processes. A PKE is the deployment of a Personal Web used to build knowledge in relation to specific learning goals, in a time dedicated to learning, centred on a user/learner and connected to other users, allowing to realise a personalised view of the learning flow, provided it is used with proper competences and method.

Wild, Modritscher, & Sigurdarson (2008) define Mash-Up Personal Learning Environment (MUPPLE) as a technological framework enabling learners to build up their own PLEs by composing Web-based tools into a single user experience, get involved in collaborative activities, share their designs with peers and adapt their designs to reflect their experience of the learning process. This framework is meant to be a generic platform for end-user development of PLEs taking into account the paradigm shift from expert-driven personalisation of learning to a design for emergence method for building a PLE.

In this research, a PLE is a concept rather than specific software, a group of techniques and a variety of tools to gather information, explore and develop relationships between pieces of information (Leone & Guazzaroni, 2010). A PLE helps to view the subject as a landscape as well as individual pieces of information; to create a personal repository of materials and relationships clustered around a unifying topic or concept; to document, reflect, communicate, collaborate. Information and knowledge reside in digital sources (locally produced files and notes, Internet/Intranet, e-learning courses, reference sites, text/audio/video/graphics files, shared presentations, RSS feeds) and in non-digital sources (books and journals, classroom-based courses, professional meetings, live interaction with colleagues). A PLE, at the same time, develops and is fed by autonomy, pragmatics, relevance, building on prior knowledge, goal-directed approach (Leone, 2009).

1.3.3   The Shift from Organisation-Centred to Learner-Centred Learning Environments. A Learning Theory for Adult Lifelong Learners

At a basic level, personalising learning entails more responsive teaching to meet students' needs; at the most profound level, personalising learning concerns self-organisation by individuals working with the support and advisory systems provided by professionals (Leadbeater, 2004); not only the process, content and assessment are negotiable with learners but the very aims and purposes of the education in which learners are engaged. Since knowledge dissemination facilitates dynamic, adaptive and personalised experiences, individuals, in their numerous roles (as citizens, customers, students and Internet users), no longer accept pre-packaged "products". Today's learners are informed, digitally literate and constantly connected; they are approaching work and learning differently, through massive connections to other people and resources, globally. In this sense, learning networks resemble ecologies (Leone & Guazzaroni, 2010).

On these premises, contemporary mainstream education seems inadequate to grasp multidimensional and planetary realities. Developing learning ecologies (Siemens, 2006) or learning habitats (Cormier 2008), atelier learning (Seely-Brown 2009), studio learning (Fisher 2008), is a first, important step toward a more general culture of learning (Seely-Brown, 1999) and, thus, toward LLL. Learning might be seen as a *learning adventure* rather than *learning work* (Leo et al., 2010), that is as a learner-centred, holistic experience which involves a complex, continual, chaotic and co-creative process.

In terms of teaching and learning, learner-centred and learner-led learning have been at the heart of many of the developments involving technology, and e-learning has become strategic.

Today designing online adult education means being able to build courses that favour generative learning, by shifting from a teacher-centred approach to a learner-centred one, from a linear learning system to a networked one, from an individual vision to a cooperative one, from a fixed programme to a project to be organised (Leone, 2009). Networked learning, variously underpinned by construc-tivism, socio-constructivism or connectivism, is manifested in PLEs (Drexler, 2010) and exploits ICT to facilitate connections: between learners, learners and tutors, a learning community and its learning resources (Steeples & Jones, 2002). It is the fusion of these connections that provides the most powerful learning potential (Goodyear, 2005).

Especially within university educational environments, the aim is to move towards more effective learning approaches (McAuliffe, Hargreaves, Winter, & Chadwick, 2009), such as andragogy (Knowles, 1970) and heutagogy (Hase & Kenyon, 2000).

Whereas pedagogy is a teaching theory, that is aiming at filling deficits in stu-dents' knowledge and comprehension of their environment, andragogy is a learning theory based on transaction, that is teacher-facilitated and addressing the immedi-ate, practical needs of context-dependent learners (McAuliffe et al., 2009).

In Knowles' andragogical model, learners are self-directed; enter educational programmes with a great diversity of experience; become ready to learn when they experience a need to know or do something; are life-centred, task-centred or problem-centred and are motivated by internal self-esteem, recognition, better qual-ity of life and self-actualisation. These principles identify and allow for differences in the adult learner's profile and goals, and in the learning context.

Still, Wheeler (2011a) sustains that the theory of andragogy (Knowles, 1970) adds very little to the current understanding of learning. Somehow, andragogy seems outmoded in the light of recent rapid change in technology-enhanced teach-ing and learning approaches. Hase and Kenyon (2000) argued that andragogy keeps a teacher–learner relationship and that in a highly technical society learning should be more self-determined. These authors made a step forward in this direction by identifying heutagogy as a desire to make the learning experience a more holistic development of the learner's capability for questioning his/her values and assumptions against the critical role of the system–environment interface (McAuliffe et al., 2009). Heutagogy sustains that individuals have the potential to learn continuously by interacting with their environment; they can learn throughout their life, develop their creativity and thus relearn how to learn. These concepts recall Rogers' view (1983), according to which human beings are constructive in nature and make every effort to realise and express their "experiencing organism".

On this basis, Wheeler (2011a) looks at heutagogy (Hase & Kenyon, 2000) and paragogy (Corneli & Danoff, 2011) as effective approaches in authentic learning contexts (Brown, Collins, & Duguid, 1989) and as more appropriate ways of framing learning in the digital age. Heutagogic learning is at its most informal and might be pictured of as a form of *flâneurism* (after Charles Baudelaire), that is the learner's act of wandering seemingly aimlessly around the digital landscape to more fully perceive it (Wheeler, 2011a).

McAuliffe et al. (2009) stress, instead, that if on one side heutagogy potentially empowers the learner more than andragogy and pedagogy do, on the other the removal of the teacher/facilitator makes the concept of heutagogy impractical in formal and non-formal learning. This confirms the validity of Knowles' theory of negotiated reality between the teacher, the student and the learning material.

The teacher is necessary to help the learners navigate the breadth of content, apply the tools properly and offer support in the form of digital literacy skills and subject matter expertise. Yet, the teacher may not be the only expert in the learning process. The ability to locate expertise beyond formal settings is one powerful benefit of a well-structured PLE (Drexler, 2010). In this perspective, networked learning opens to paragogy (Corneli & Danoff, 2011) as a renewed descriptive framework of peer-to-peer learning, where students support each other's learning on an equal basis. In this sense, paragogy is an extension of the concept of scaffolding (Bruner, 1960), where knowledgeable others (teachers or peers) as learners connect with each other, share their content and ideas and engage in dialogue (Wheeler, 2011a). Paragogy may also find more synergy than andragogy with other theoretical approaches for co-constructed and networked learning, such as constructivism (Barr & Tagg, 1995; Jonassen & Land, 2000; Von Glasersfeld, 1998), socio-constructivism (Varisco, 2002; Vygotsky, 1986) and connectivism (Downes, 2006; Siemens, 2004).

The learning that is made possible by social software tools is active, process-based, experiential (Kolb, 1984), anchored in and driven by learners' interests, and therefore has the potential to cultivate self-regulated, independent learning (McLoughlin & Lee, 2010). Self-regulation relates to an ability to recognise a need for further learning as well as to be proactive in gaining access to and accomplishing learning (Leone, 2010). A self-regulated learner is able to adapt his/her approach to learning, to regulate his/her performance along with how he/she learns (i.e. metaknowledge) (Winne, 1997; Zimmerman, 1990) and to execute learning activities that lead to knowledge creation, comprehension and higher order learning (Stubbé & Theunissen, 2008) by using processes such as monitoring, reflection, testing, questioning and self-evaluation. In addition, self-regulation works best when learners are provided with continuing feedback concerning the effectiveness of their learning approach (Zimmerman, 1990). Lifelong learners are self-regulated learners.

All this is possible if to the two levels of planning, teaching planning of modular learning objects and technological planning of the communication environment, a third level is added, that is, informal e-learning.

The adoption of online learning tools and methods should be preceded by the harmonisation of formal teaching spaces with the spaces agreed in the learning communities. Formal teaching spaces are defined within LMSs. Spaces agreed in the learning communities, instead, are to be used by social software (dynamic platforms, blogs, wikis, e-mails). They are aimed to build networks of virtual identities and to define PLEs of dynamic contents, based on continuous accesses, validations, dialogic exchanges. As a consequence, the process by which technologies, used by communication experts, impose learning within prescribed interactions is inverted; social software allows the learner to the fundamental use of technologies as means to represent, connect and express his/her knowledge; Web 2.0 technologies and tools facilitate learning ecologies. E-learning 2.0, in particular, has mediated the shift from formal to informal e-learning (Leone, 2009; Sclater, 2008; Trentin, 2005), from Virtual Learning Environments (VLEs), which are organisation-centred spaces (Bonaiuti, 2007), to PLEs as emerging learner-centred spaces (Rogers, 1983; Vygotsky, 1986).

Even though universities still tend to rely on conservative, established VLEs, recent reports from various countries including the UK (see Bryant, 2007; CLEX, 2009; Minocha, 2009; Owen, Grant, Sayers, & Facer, 2006), USA (see New Media Consortium, 2009; Salaway, Caruso, & Nelson, 2008) and Australia (see Fitzgerald & Steele, 2008) point out that the integration of social software into formal learning environments can make a qualitative difference to giving students a sense of ownership and control over their own learning and career planning (McLoughlin & Lee, 2010).

A decade ago, VLEs were the main setting of e-learning. Over recent years, however, as a result of the growing adoption of a LLL approach, traditional VLE has shown the following weaknesses:

- the focus on the creation on rigid schemes, blocks and platforms, which engenders the lack of sharing and common spaces;
- asymmetric relations and the consequent limited production of contents according to the participants' roles (teachers/learners);
- the lack of adoption of open and simple standards (e.g. RSS);
- a poor interaction with the community external to the learning environment, in terms of visibility of the outcomes of the learning process and lack of access to the contents—not even to the alumni;
- impeded construction of the individual's virtual identity (crucial aim in LLL policies);

Dequalification of the learning community and scanty interrelation among different education contexts are the evident consequences. The ongoing change of perspective has brought attention on the framework of the learner-centred approach as a new alternative to traditional VLE (Giovannella, 2008):

- the Web used as a platform or an environment, where various tools and contents can be aggregated for the construction of a PLE;
- socially constructed educational materials;
- symmetric relations (active role for all the participants);
- open source, open content, open society and, as a result, adoption of open "machine-readable" standards interconnected with proprietary ones;
- the learner's capability of managing his/her learning processes and of configurating his/her e-portfolio as aggregator of personal knowledge and competences (Lubesky, 2006);
- social interaction as a means to learn, to co-construct knowledge and to communicate.

It's no more the user who adapts to the learning environment, but it's the education system that designs learning environments on the learner's needs and prior knowledge. Besides, individuals are more and more oriented to build their own PLE.

The comparison between VLE and PLE points out how the latter is more adherent to the users' expectations of flexibility, active participation and individualisation of a learning environment (Calvani, Buonaiuti, Fini, & Ranieri, 2007; Downes, 2006); rather PLE is the new learning setting to look at (Attwell, 2007). Nonetheless, if the learner-centred model is adopted in VLEs (Anderson, 2006), the two settings can be synergic and can be interconnected through knowledge-sharing technologies, like RSS.

A third alternative between organisation-centred VLE and user-centred PLE could be Learning Places (LP) (Giovannella, 2008), settings that are opened to the interaction with the outside and attentive to the development of individuals' virtual identity. Leo et al. (2010) propose a Personal Knowledge Space (PKS) as a specific implementation of the PLE approach in a formal learning setting, that is as an evolution or an integration of the VLE. The PKS would be the teacher-facilitated environment where learners can manage knowledge, exploiting some features of Web 2.0 within the formal setting. The PKS would be developed on an adaptive modular, flexible and interoperable architecture.

Indeed, we are witnessing the passage from a Cartesian view of learning (knowledge as substance and pedagogy as knowledge transfer) to a social view of learning (understanding is socially constructed and participating builds up identity) (Seely-Brown, 2009).

1.3.4   Implicit and Explicit Personalisation of Learning: Adaptive Mechanisms and Social Semantic Web

Personalised advanced e-learning environments bring into focus the student as the main actor of the learning process.

Both the terms personalisation and customisation have been increasingly considered as key components of Web applications and refer to using information about a user to provide tailored products and services more effectively (Kramer, Noronha, & Vergo, 2000), but the two notions differ in several respects. More specifically, personalisation is a toolbox of technologies and application features used in the design of an end-user experience, and it is automatically performed by a Web site based on the history of previous interactions with the user, on the user's profile or on like-minded users' profiles. Customisation, instead, is usually used to describe the interface attributes that are user-controlled (i.e. user's configuration of a Web site, a product or a service according to personal preferences and requirements); the system is almost passive and provides only a means by which the configuration is set (Braynov, 2004).

Accordingly, data for the user's profiling can be collected implicitly or explicitly. Implicit profiling is automatically carried out by the system by tracking and monitoring users' behaviour in order to identify browsing or buying patterns. Explicit collection, instead, usually requires the user's active participation, thereby allowing the user to control the information in his/her profile and to express directly needs and modalities. A combination of implicit and explicit profiling allows to obtain a hybrid method of personalisation.

Web personalisation is closely linked to the notion of Adaptive Hypermedia (AH), that is a system that tailors the selection of links or contents to be visualised on the user's goals, abilities, interests, knowledge, context, device used to access the information (e.g. handheld device, laptop, desktop, etc.).

A very popular (and historically the first) application field of AH is Adaptive Educational Hypermedia (AEH), which "adapts" the learning path to the learner's profile (Brusilovsky, 1998). Additionally, the term *intelligent tutoring (or educational) systems* is widely used in the educational domain. Intelligent tutoring systems focus on the use of techniques from the field of artificial intelligence to provide broader and better support for the learners. In contrast, adaptive educational systems stress the aim to be different for different learners or groups of learners (Brusilovsky & Peylo, 2003). However, many systems can be considered as intelligent and adaptive educational systems (Graf, 2007).

The spectrum of adaptation in systems ranges from adaptive systems to adaptable systems (Oppermann, Rashev, & Kinshuk, 1997). *Adaptable systems* allow the user to change certain parameters and adapt the systems' behaviour accordingly. In contrast, *adaptive systems* adapt to the users, automatically based on the system's assumptions about the users' needs (Oppermann, 1994).

More in detail, the classification of adaptive systems on basis of authority includes five categories (Fig. 1.8) (Oppermann & Simm, 1994) based on information the user is given about the systems status, and how much control the machine and the user have over the initiation of the adaptation:

- *adaptive*. The machine has total control over adaptation;
- *system-initiated adaptivity*. The machine will notify the user of any changes prior to their execution. The operator still has no control over the choice, timing or implementation of adaptation;

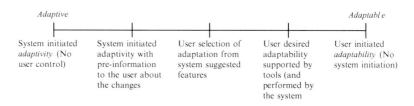

Fig. 1.8 Spectrum of adaptivity (Oppermann & Simm, 1994)

- *operator selected adaptation*. Using suggestions from the machine, the user selects the adaptation. The machine still performs the action;
- *operator-initiated adaptability*: The user chooses and initiates the adaptation, without any suggestions from the machine, but the machine implements the change;
- *adaptable*. The user is in complete control of adaptation.

In adaptive learning systems, adaptivity consists in increased user's efficiency, effectiveness and satisfaction by greater correspondence between learner, goal and characteristics of the system. Adaptivity applies when (1) users generally work on their own without external support; (2) the system is used by a variety of users from all over the world (different learning approaches, cultures and background); (3) customised system behaviour reduces meta-learning overhead for the user and allows focus on completion of actual task (Graf, Lan, Liu, & Kinshuk (2009).

Modelling the learner's characteristics is determinant for systems providing adaptivity or personalisation (Graf, Lin, Jeffrey, & Kinshuk, 2006). The user model, a main component of any adaptive system, contains information about an individual user's knowledge, goals and preferences, and allows adaptive systems to use this information accordingly (Brusilovsky, Kobsa, & Nejdl, 2007). Indeed, learners' needs must be detected before adaptivity can be supplied (Graf & Kinshuk, 2006). Brusilovsky (1996) mentioned two different approaches for obtaining information about a learner's needs (1) the collaborative student modelling approach, by which learners provide explicit information about themselves by filling out a questionnaire; (2) the automatic student modelling approach, by which the system monitors the learners' actions and behaviour and infers their needs automatically while they are learning within the system.

Normally, adaptive learning systems lack support for teachers, apart from providing basic functions, and require educational designers to create their courses based on quite strict rules and predefined types of learning objects (LOs). If few of the required types of LOs are not included (e.g. because they are not relevant to the learning path), the adaptivity is strongly affected or might not work at all (Graf et al., 2010). This might be one of the reasons why adaptive systems are rarely used in educational institutions.

Most of the adaptive mechanisms operate upon the assessment of learners' prior and progressively acquired knowledge. Some, though, are based on learners' learning styles as well (Alfonseca, Carro, Martin, Ortigosa, & Paredes, 2006; Sangineto, Capuano, Gaeta, & Micarelli, 2008).

Graf and Kinshuk (2007) focused on enhancing LMSs' functionality with adaptivity based on students' learning styles, and developed, implemented and successfully evaluated an adaptive mechanism that was based on changing the sequence and number of six types of LOs when presenting them to students that learn differently.

In a more recent work, Graf et al. (2010) improved this system and introduced a flexible adaptive mechanism for LMSs, with respect to the LOs provided. The authors used adaptive sorting and adaptive annotation in order to highlight the LOs that support students' learning process the best. Teachers can freely choose from many different types of LOs foreseen by the mechanism to be included in one or more sections of a course. In this study, the authors considered 12 types of LOs; however, new ones can easily be included, if required, thus making the mechanism a novel flexible and extendable adaptive framework that does not limit the richness of the learning resources and materials. In this regard, this adaptive system is different from others and can, therefore, be favourably considered by more educational institutions (Graf et al., 2010).

Limongelli, Sciarrone, Temperini, and Vaste (2009) devised another framework for personalisation and adaptation in e-learning, LS-Plan, in which an adaptation engine spawns and continuously adjusts personalised courses from repositories of learning nodes, through an adaptation algorithm and a planner based on linear temporal logic. In this mechanism, adaptation works upon entry and ongoing learners' knowledge and learning styles.

The authors carried out an extensive experimental evaluation by integrating LS-Plan in an educational hypermedia, the Lecomps Web application (Limongelli et al., 2009), and more recently in Moodle,[5] creating the Moodle_LS system (Limongelli, Sciarrone, & Vaste, 2011), to deliver several personalised courses on *Italian Neorealist Cinema*.

A common view among researchers is that, even though LMSs offer flexible and modular technology-enhanced learning, by providing a great variety of learning resources and activities which teachers can easily include in their courses (e.g. learning materials, quizzes, forums, chats, assignments, wikis, etc.), they deliver identical structure, composition and content of a course for every learner (Bonaiuti, 2007; Giovannella, 2008; Graf et al., 2010; Limongelli et al., 2011; McLoughlin & Lee, 2010). In particular, Limongelli et al. (2011) sustain that Moodle's potential in personalising learning is restricted; some personalisation features are available for the user interface (i.e. it is possible to personalise the environment by creating new themes) and some by the implementation of plug-ins from the Moodle official Web site. Moodle 2.0 appears more flexible in the definition of alternative learning paths thanks to the *conditional activities*, that is activities that can be made available to the learner according to certain conditions (e.g. grade obtained in one or more tests, completion of one or more activities or a combination of the two). Limongelli et al. (2011), however, are convinced that teachers remain in charge of defining possible alternative learning paths.

---

[5]Martin Dougiamas's Modular Object Oriented Dynamic Learning Environment (http://www.moodle.org) is one of the most widely used LMSs in the world, by over 31 million students in over 44,000 sites in over 200 countries (Cooch, 2010).

In contrast with this point of view, Cooch (2010) extensively exemplifies how Moodle 2.0 allows to personalise learning by fully exploiting conditional activities[6] and the *activity completion tracking* facility.

No research literature nor mention in the Moodle community, anyhow, seems to be available about the implementation of Moodle 2.0 conditional activities in learning paths for adult lifelong learners.

Moodle's design and development draws upon social constructionist philosophy.[7] This implies that Moodle is devised particularly for teachers who facilitate their students' learning, rather than lecture to them; for learners to be in charge of their own learning, discussing, collaborating and actively "constructing" their own knowledge; for learners to find their own path, rather than to follow a path set down for them by someone else. Nevertheless, Moodle 2.0 also allows the implementation of different degrees of learning personalisation between the following extremes (a) teachers can choose to roughly guide students, by scaffolding, and let them find their own way; (b) teachers can choose to give them a detailed map with checkpoints they must reach along the way, that is a more structured approach. Further, the determination of learners' learning styles is possible by creating a suitable quiz or, for Moodle 1.9, by adding a special plug-in.[8]

Both Graf et al.'s (2010) and Limongelli et al.'s (2011) frameworks adopted the Felder and Silverman's (1988) model to detect students' learning styles. Many other learning style models exist in literature, such as Kolb's (1984), Honey and Mumford's (1982) and Pask's (1976) models. While there are still several open issues with respect to learning styles (Coffield, Moseley, Hall, & Ecclestone, 2004; Graf et al., 2010; Litzinger, Lee, Wise, & Felder, 2007), all models concur that learners have different ways in which they prefer to learn. Besides, numerous researchers sustain that learning styles are important factors as potential facilitators of the learning process (Graf et al., 2010). Several evaluations of adaptive systems that incorporate learning styles have confirmed this point, showing that adaptivity based on learning styles can lead to less time required for learning and higher overall learner satisfaction (Graf & Kinshuk, 2007; Popescu, 2008; Tseng, Chu, Hwang, & Tsai, 2008).

In this research, the Felder–Silverman learning styles model (FSLSM) (Felder & Silverman, 1988) is adopted. FSLSM describes a learner's learning style in very much detail, assuming that each learner has a preference on each of the four dimensions (1) active/reflective, (2) sensing/intuitive, (3) visual/verbal and (4) sequential/global, with assignable values on a -11 to $+11$ scale. By using dimensions instead of types and a numerical evaluation, the strengths of students' preference for a determined learning style can be evidenced; besides, the FSLSM is based on tendencies,

---

[6]A workaround to controlling students' access was made available for Moodle 1.9: *activity locking* was a means whereby a teacher could set certain conditions on a task that a learner had to meet before the next task became visible. With Moodle 2.0 this feature is standard, by conditional activities (Cooch, 2010).

[7]http://docs.moodle.org/en/Philosophy.

[8]http://moodle.org/mod/forum/discuss.php?d=140054.

and thus allows to consider exceptional behaviour. Furthermore, several researchers concur on the validity of the FSLSM as the most appropriate model to be used in adaptive learning systems (Carver, Howard, & Lane, 1999; Graf et al., 2010; Kuljis & Liu, 2005; Limongelli et al., 2011).

1.3.5 From the Social Web to the Social Semantic Web

In the vision of supporting the characterisation of lifelong learners' PLEs, the diffused adoption of LMSs enhanced with adaptive mechanisms in formal learning could be a first outstanding change. At the same time, though, informal learning should be integrated as a smooth continuum by social software, in order to use Web 2.0 technologies and tools as means to represent, connect and express individuals' knowledge, that is to facilitate learning ecologies (Leone, 2009).

The progression from the network as information provider (Web 1.0) to the network as platform (Web 2.0), introduced by O'Reilly (2005), has brought about a new technological paradigm (Gaballo, 2007). The shift from Web 1.0, "the original Web", to Web 2.0, the Web of social networking tools, has created unique and powerful information sharing and collaboration features. Current generations have witnessed the evolution from simple Web sites that were largely read-only to read–write ones, from centralization of information to decentralisation and spreading of knowledge. Contents and competences are no more delivered through a top-down education process, but they are created and used through a bottom-up procedure, through symmetric interaction and real-time information and through the millions of blogs and posts which are present in the universe of bits of the World Wide Web (Leone & Guazzaroni, 2010).

This is the Social Web, differently defined as expression of collective intelligence (Levy, 1997) or of wisdom of crowds (Surowiecki, 2004), as an ecosystem of participation where value is created by the aggregation of many individual users' contributions that results in *collected* intelligence (Gruber, 2008), rather than collective intelligence. In Gruber's view, collective intelligence implies the emergence of truly new levels of understanding from the recombination of the data gathered, and has to be a scientific and societal goal to be achieved through the Internet. The Semantic Web, an ecosystem of data, where value is created by the integration of structured data from many sources (Gruber, 2008), is the other key element of this evolution. Tim Berners-Lee's "Semantic" Web is not "a separate Web"; it is "an extension of the current one" where information is attributed "well-defined meaning, better enabling computers and people to work in cooperation" (Berners-Lee, Handler, & Lassila, 2001).

In adherence to this strategic vision, the Social Web and the Semantic Web are merging into the Social Semantic Web, that is going to encompass the creation of explicit and semantically rich knowledge representations as a result of developments in social interactions, opening up for a more social interface to the semantics. As a whole, the Social Semantic Web can be considered as a Web of *collective knowledge systems* (Gruber, 2008), human–computer systems, a Web which aims to integrate the formal frame of the Semantic Web with a pragmatic approach based on description codes for semantic browsing using heuristic classification and semiotic ontologies.

Structured and unstructured, formal and informal are poles of a continuum. To get better reasoning, better data have to be gathered and represented in a more complex way. The core of a social semantic system is a continuous process of eliciting key knowledge of a field through semi-formal ontologies, taxonomies or folksonomies (Leone & Guazzaroni, 2010), exploiting the connections between people and their objects of interest.

Also, to better enable user access to multiple sites, interoperability among Social Web sites is required in terms of both the expressed data (content objects, person-to-person networks, etc.) and the social applications in use (e.g. widgets) on each site. This requires representation mechanisms for data and applications on the Social Web in an interoperable and extensible way. The Semantic Web provides such representation mechanisms: It can be used to link people and objects by expressing the heterogeneous ties that bind individuals to each other (either explicitly or implicitly) (Breslin, Passant, & Decker, 2009).

In a LLL scenario, the potential is evident. Knowledge is enriched by the integrations of different perspectives (Downes, 2006), and relevant knowledge is involved with complexity (Leone & Guazzaroni, 2010). Lifelong learners growingly use social search to find relevant results from their network, trusting more results that are already recommended by their peers. Learners use tags both to classify their content and to find interesting resources and users with common interests. The learner might establish relations with these users. If these relations are unidirectional, the learner is a user's "fan" or "follower" or "subscriber", that is the learner is interested in what the user posts on the Web site. If these relations are bidirectional, the learner and the user are "friends", that is they both acknowledge the existence of a relationship, or they both are interested in the other's activities on the Web site. These connections let learners monitor new resources appearing on the network from relevant users and discover new valuable connections from the users' peers. However, these connections become really valuable only if and when they entail a growing and updated network of trusted learning sources efficiently. This can take place through the use of Social Semantic Web tools.

Semantic Web vocabularies such as FOAF (Friend of a Friend), SIOC (Semantically Interlinked Online Communities) and MOAT (Meaning Of A Tag) provide rich features that can be used to represent and infer social actors and ties.

FOAF project (http://www.foaf-project.org) is creating a Web of machine-readable pages describing people, the links between them and the things they create and do. FOAF defines an open, decentralised technology for connecting social Web sites, and the people they describe. Specifically, foaf:knows relations can form ties in social networks on the Semantic Web by directly linking two foaf:person. FOAF has been recognised as means of sharing social network data between social networking Web sites, and the ease of producing Semantic Web data is promoting this evolution (Zhou, Ding, & Finin, 2011).

The SIOC initiative (http://sioc-project.org/) aims to enable the integration of online community information. SIOC provides a Semantic Web ontology for representing rich data from the Social Web in RDF. It is commonly used in conjunction with the FOAF vocabulary for expressing personal profile and social networking information. By becoming a standard way for expressing user-generated content from such sites, SIOC enables new kinds of usage scenarios for online community site data, and allows innovative semantic applications to be built on top of the existing Social Web.

MOAT (http://moat-project.org/) provides a Semantic Web framework to publish semantically enriched content from free-tagging one, providing a way for users to define meaning(s) of their tag(s) using URIs of Semantic Web resources. Thanks to those relationships between tags and URIs of existing concepts, they can annotate content with those URIs rather than free-text tags, leveraging content into Semantic Web, by linking data together. Moreover, these tag meanings can be shared between people, providing an architecture of participation to define and exchange meanings of tags (as URIs) within a community of users.

In addition to these vocabularies, embeddable application widgets on Social Web sites enable these sites to interoperate by appealing to some common semantics. A social aspect can be added to data (e.g. software project and widgets descriptions), so that social networking, trust and relationship aspects can be combined with those representation models.

Recently various research projects funded by the EU have been carried out to provide networked and personalised learning environments for lifelong learners,[9] but a few have investigated new applications that exploit Social Semantic Web to enhance LLL, like Learning Technologies for Lifelong Learning (LTfLL)[10] and Responsive Open Learning Environments (ROLE).[11] In the following, the most relevant LTfLL tools are detailed.

Within the LTfLL project, the Common Semantic Framework (CSF) supports stakeholders in identifying, retrieving and exchanging the relevant learning material for a given learning task. The CSF includes Formal and Informal Learning Support Systems.

The Formal Learning Support System (FLSS) offers teachers and students access to learning materials via semantic search techniques. A simple text search returns documents with a varying degree of relevance, by using different wordings of a concept and exploiting implicit semantic relations in the text. The system data

---

[9]See http://cordis.europa.eu/fp6/projects.htm and http://cordis.europa.eu/fp7/projects_en.html.

[10]LTfLL (http://www.ltfll-project.org/index.php/index.html) was co-funded by the EU under the ICT theme, 7th Framework Programme for R&D (FP7-ICT-2007-1-4.1) (2008–2011). It aimed to provide personalised formative feedback for facilitating formal collaborative learning and informal social learning, finding innovative ways to the challenges of pervasive technology-enhanced learning: gaining access to the right tools, mastering them, usability and optimised utilisation, interoperability, content overload.

[11]ROLE (http://www.role-project.eu/) is supported by the EC, in ICT-2007 Digital Libraries and technology-enhanced learning, 7th Framework Programme (2009–2013). It is a European collaborative project (16 research groups from 6 EU countries and China) whose main task is to deliver and test prototypes of highly responsive PLEs, offering breakthrough levels of effectiveness, flexibility, user-control and mass-individualisation.

include a domain ontology to provide a formal conceptualization of a domain and semantically annotated LOs. The services provide search, edit and visualisation facilities to help the user access and modify the information; the user can also leave comments and remarks.

Validation results have shown that the high proportion of learning materials in FLSS are relevant for the course creation. Semantic search is the service that facilitates the retrieval of relevant materials with respect to a specific topic. Also, the ontology as a structured resource helps the tutors in designing their courses. Nevertheless, some requirements still lack for the smooth adoption of FLSS (1) addition of new learning materials and modification of ontologies in the system; (2) better highlighting of the data within the system; (3) documentation (exhaustive guidelines and use cases).[12]

The Informal Learning Support System (iFLSS) consists of a range of services that support knowledge retrieval through an ontology enhanced with the vocabulary of the Community of Practice (CoP) and by recommending material on the basis of the content, tags and users belonging to the CoP (Monachesi, Markus, Westerhout, Osenova, & Simov, 2011). The system is based on a domain ontology enrichment methodology, word sense disambiguation and semantic modelling of social media content (Monachesi & Markus, 2010). The widget-based visualisation of the system has a strong focus towards using an expert validated ontology for providing a structured overview of the domain, while social media services allow for personalisation of content recommendation (Posea & Trausan-Matu, 2010). Communication is facilitated through the use of social networks, and new communities of learners can be established through the recommendations provided by the system.

The iFLSS process can be described as follows. The learner has to find relevant content for his learning task. He can use the ontology browsing functionality of the CSF to improve his/her knowledge on the domain of the topic. The learner can also use this browsing functionality to retrieve documents. In addition to the browsing-based search, the learner can search for relevant materials in two other ways. The first option is to employ semantic search on the basis of the domain ontology. The second search functionality is based on the structure of the social network and the tags attached to resources. In addition to the document itself, the retrieved results indicate the peers associated with these resources which are part of his/her social network, enabling the learner to contact these persons. The result of this search is trusted because it has the guarantee of a peer recommendation. The different search possibilities are all available and the learner can freely switch to one another, according to his/her needs. The ontology, tags, annotations and links to resources are stored in the semantic repository (Posea & Trausan-Matu, 2010).

Validation results have confirmed that the iFLSS knowledge discovery and social search systems provide a high proportion of relevant learning materials that match the search topic. Anyhow, since the software was designed for a self-directed LLL

---

[12]See Deliverable D2.5–LTfLL Roadmap at http://www.ltfll-project.org/index.php/deliverables.html.

context but during the project the validation was aimed at an academic institution with a fixed curriculum, an additional validation activity would need to be run in order to verify whether the software better addresses the needs of such learners or whether other requirements arise when used with another type of learners. Additionally, a less elaborate method for setting up the system and an installation guide needs to be provided (Westerhout, Monachesi, Markus, & Posea, 2010).

Learners, guided by a domain ontology, were able to retrieve relevant learning materials from Delicious, YouTube, Bibsonomy and Slideshare. In addition, they could filter the results of their search by looking at their own social network.

1.4   Summary

As a whole, this chapter has allowed to achieve the following results. The diffusing LLL vision, emerging practices with social semantic computing technologies and research findings signal that learning occurs for the most part outside the traditional formal situations, especially for adult lifelong learners. Lifelong learners are self-regulated learners who need to be supported in gaining control over the learning process as a whole, and in pursuing personal life goals and needs. Thus, more personal, social and participatory frameworks have to be adopted.

Since in relation to personalisation of learning most LMSs are weak, recently some researchers have successfully implemented adaptive plug-ins in Moodle 1.9, in which adaptivity is based on the detection of learners' learning styles by the FSLSM as the most acknowledged model in this kind of application. Anyhow, no similar research experiences seem to have been developed with Moodle 2.0 yet; further, none of the adaptive plug-ins that have been reported in this chapter have been adapted to Moodle 2.0 yet, nor have been devised learning formats that exploit Moodle 2.0 conditional activities as an adaptive mechanism.

The dichotomy LMS vs. PLE can be transformed into models of integration on the background of a student-centred framework, provided an attentive design of the underlying technological architecture that is accessible to both teachers and learners. In particular, knowledge management, trustworthiness and assessment on the collection of resources and personalisation issues call for a thorough analysis of suitable Social Semantic Web tools to be adopted within the integrated learning environment.

References

Alberici, A., Catarsi, C., Colapietro, V., & Loiodice, I. (2007). *Adulti e Università Sfide ed innovazioni nella formazione universitaria e continua*. Milano: Franco Angeli.

Alfonseca, E., Carro, R. M., Martin, E., Ortigosa, A., & Paredes, P. (2006). The impact of learning styles on student grouping for collaborative learning: A case study. *User Modelling and User-Adapted Interaction, 16*, 377–401.

Anderson, P. (2006). *What is Web 2.0? Ideas, technologies and implications for education*. JISC. Retrieved May 12, 2011 from http://www.ukoln.ac.uk/terminolgy/JISC-review2006.html

Attwell, G. (2007). *Personal learning environments - the future of eLearning?* eLearning Papers 2. Retrieved May 12, 2011 from http://www.elearningeuropa.info/out/?doc_id=9758&rsr_id=11561

Attwell, G. (2008). The social impact of personal learning environments. In S. Wheeler (Ed.), *Connected minds, emerging cultures: Cybercultures in online learning*. Charlotte, NC: Information Age.

Barr, R., & Tagg, J. (1995). From teaching to learning: A new paradigm for undergraduate education. *Change Magazine, 2*, 8–12.

Bentley, T. (2005). *Personalised learning in the UK: from vision to strategy?* Personalised learning: high expectations symposium. Sydney (NSW): Department of Education and Training.

Bentley, T., & Miller, R. (2004). *Personalised learning: Creating the ingredients for system and society-wide change*. Melbourne: IARTV Incorporated Association of Registered Teachers of Victoria.

Berners-Lee, T., Handler, J., & Lassila, O. (2001). The semantic Web. *Scientific American.* Retrieved September 23, 2008 from http://www.ryerson.ca/~dgrimsha/courses/cps720_02/resources/Scientific%20American%20The%20Semantic%20Web.htm

Bloom, B. S. (Ed.). (1985). *Developing talent in young people*. New York: Ballentine Books.

Bonaiuti, G. (2007). *I learning object nella prospettiva dell"eLearning 2.0*. Atti del IV congresso Sie-l.

Braynov, S. (2004). Personalization and customization technologies. *The Internet Encyclopedia.* Retrieved May 15, 2011 from http://onlinelibrary.wiley.com/doi/10.1002/047148296X.tie141/full

Breslin, J., Passant, A., & Decker, S. (2009). *The social semantic Web*. Berlin: Springer.

Broek, S. D., & Buiskool, B. J. (2010). *Key competences for adult learning professionals*. Zetermeer: Research voor Beleid.

Brown, J. S., Collins, A., & Duguid, P. (1989). Situated cognition and the culture of learning. *Educational Researcher, 18*, 32–42.

Bruner, J. (1960). *The process of education*. Cambridge, MA: Harvard University Press.

Brusilovsky, P. (1996). Methods and techniques of adaptive hypermedia. *Journal of User Modelling and User Adaptation Interaction, 6*, 87–129.

Brusilovsky, P. (1998). Adaptive educational systems on the World-Wide-Web. In G. Ayala (Ed.), *Current trends and applications of artificial intelligence in education* (pp. 9–16). Proceedings of Workshop at the 4th World Congress on Expert Systems, ITESM, Mexico City, Mexico.

Brusilovsky, P., Kobsa, A., & Nejdl, W. (2007). The adaptive Web: Methods and strategies of Web personalization. In *Lecture Notes in Computer Sciences*. Berlin: Springer.

Brusilovsky, P., & Peylo, C. (2003). Adaptive and intelligent Web-based educational systems. *International Journal of Artificial Intelligence in Education, 13*, 156–169.

Bryant, L. (2007). Emerging trends in social software for education. In *Emerging technologies for learning* (Vol. 2, pp. 10–18). Coventry, UK: Becta.

Calvani, A. (2006). *Reti, comunità e conoscenza Costruire e gestire dinamiche collaborative*. Trento: Erikson.

Calvani, A., Buonaiuti, G., Fini, A., & Ranieri, M. (2007). *I Personal Learning Environment: una chiave di volta per il Lifelong Learning?* Atti del IV congresso Sie-l

Campbell, R. J., Robinson, W., Neelands, J., Hewston, R., & Mazzoli, L. (2007). Personalised learning: Ambiguities in theory and practice. *British Journal of Educational Studies, 55*, 135–154.

Carver, C. A., Howard, R. A., & Lane, W. D. (1999). Addressing different learning styles through course hypermedia. *IEEE Transactions on Education, 42*, 33–38.

Cedefop. (2011). *Lifelong guidance across Europe: Reviewing policy progress and future prospects*. Luxembourg: Publications Office of the European Union.

Chatti, M. A., Agustiawan, M. R., Jarke, M., & Specht, M. (2010). Toward a personal learning environment framework. *International Journal of Virtual and Personal Learning Environments, 1*, 66–85.

Claparède, E. (1920). *L'école sur mesure*. Genève: Payot.

CLEX. (2009). *Higher education in a Web 2.0 world: Report of an independent Committee of Inquiry into the impact on higher education of students' widespread use of Web 2.0 technologies*. Bristol: CLEX.

Coffield, F., Moseley, D., Hall, E., & Ecclestone, K. (2004). *Should we be using learning styles? What research has to say to practice*. London: Learning and Skills Research Centre/University of Newcastle upon Tyne.

Cooch, M. (2010). *Moodle 2.0 First look*. Birmingham: Packt Publishing.

Cormier, D. (2008). *Rhizomatic knowledge communities: Edtechtalk, Webcast Academy*. Dave's Educational Blog. Retrieved May 29, 2009 from http://davecormier.com/edblog/2008/02/29/rhizomatic-knowledge-communities-edtechtalk-webcast-academy/

Corneli, J., & Danoff, C. J. (2011). *Paragogy: synergizing individual and organizational learning*. Retrieved September 29, 2011 from http://en.wikiversity.org/wiki/User:Arided/ParagogyPaper

Council of the European Union. (2004). *Resolution of the Council on strengthening policies, systems and practices in the field of guidance throughout life in Europe*. Brussels: Council of the European Union.

Council of the European Union. (2008). Resolution of the Council and of the Representatives of the Governments of the Member States, meeting within the Council of 21 November 2008 on better integrating lifelong guidance into lifelong learning strategies. *Official Journal of the European Union*, 4–7.

Council of the European Union. (2010). Conclusions on the social dimension of education and training. *Official Journal of the European Union*, 2–7.

Downes, S. (2006). *Learning networks and connective knowledge*. Retrieved May 29, 2009 from http://it.coe.uga.edu/itforum/paper92/paper92.html

Downes, S. (2007). *Learning networks in practice. Emerging technologies for learning*. Retrieved May 29, 2009 from http://www.downes.ca/files/Learning_Networks_In_Practice.pdf

Downes, S. (2010). *Personal learning environments*. Retrieved May 29, 2009 from http://www.downes.ca/presentation/245

Drexler, W. (2010). The networked student model for construction of personal learning environments: Balancing teacher control and student autonomy. *Australasian Journal of Educational Technology, 26*, 369–385.

EAEA. (2006). *The common European adult learning framework*. Brussels: EAEA.

European Commission (2000). *E-learning – designing tomorrow's education*. Brussels: European Commission.

European Commission. (2001). *Making a European area of lifelong learning a reality*. Brussels: European Commission.

European Commission. (2002). *European report on quality indicators of lifelong learning*. Brussels: European Commission.

European Commission. (2006). *Communication from the Commission Adult learning: It is never too late to learn*. Brussels: European Commission.

European Commission. (2007). *Communication action plan on adult learning: It is always a good time to learn*. Brussels: European Commission.

European Commission. (2008a). *The Lifelong Learning Programme 2007–2013 Glossary*. Brussels: European Commission.

European Commission. (2008b). *Progress towards the Lisbon objectives in education and training indicators and benchmarks 2008*. Brussels: European Commission.

European Commission. (2008c). *ALPINE - Adult Learning Professions in Europe: A study of the current situation, trends and issues*. Brussels: European Commission.

European Commission. (2009). *Progress towards the Lisbon objectives in education and training indicators and benchmarks 2009*. Luxembourg: European Commission.

European Commission. (2011a). *Action plan on adult learning: Achievements and results 2008–2010*. Brussels: European Commission.

European Commission. (2011b). *Progress towards the Lisbon objectives in education and training: Indicators and benchmarks 2010/2011*. Brussels: European Commission.

European Parliament; Council of the European Union. (2006). Recommendation of the European Parliament and of the Council of 18 December 2006 on key competences for lifelong learning. *Official Journal of the European Union*, 10–18.

European Parliament; Council of the European Union. (2008). Recommendation of the European Parliament and of the Council of 23 April 2008 on the establishment of the European Qualifications Framework for lifelong learning. *Official Journal of the European Union*, 1–7.

European Parliament; Council of the European Union. (2009). Recommendation of the European Parliament and of the Council of 18 June 2009 on the establishment of a European Credit System for Vocational Education and Training (ECVET). *Official Journal of the European Union*, 11–18.

Ewing, T. (2007). The building blocks of high school redesign. *ASCD Infobrief, 49*.

FEDORA. (2007). *Charter on guidance and counselling within the European higher education area*. Brussels: FEDORA.

Felder, R. M., & Silverman, L. K. (1988). Learning and teaching styles in engineering education. *Engineering Education, 78*, 674–681.

Felder, R. M., & Soloman, B. A. (1997). *Index of learning styles questionnaire*. Retrieved August 30, 2011 from http://www.engr.ncsu.edu/learningstyles/ilsweb.html

Fisher, C. (2008). *Networks and studios*. Retrieved June 16, 2009 from http://learning2cn.ning.com/profile/ClarenceFisher

Fitzgerald, R., & Steele, J. (2008). *Digital Learning Communities (DLC): Investigating the application of social software to support networked learning (CG6-36)*. Sydney: Australian Learning and Teaching Council.

Fullan, M. (2009). *Michael Fullan's answer to "what is personalized learning?"* Microsoft Partner Network. Retrieved August 13, 2011 from http://cs.mseducommunity.com/wikis.personal.michael-fullan-s-answer-to-quot-what-is-personalized-learning-quot/revision/3.aspx

Gaballo, V. (2007). *Web 2.0 Educational eLearning and knowledge management in higher education*. Atti del IV congresso Sie-l.

Garcia Hoz, V. (1981). *Personalized education*. Valladolid: Minon. S. A.

Gardner, H. (1983). *Frames of mind: The theory of multiple intelligences*. New York: Basic Books.

Giovannella, C. (2008). *Learning 2.0?* Atti del V congresso Sie-l.

Goodyear, P. (2005). Educational design and networked learning: Patterns, pattern languages and design practice. *Australasian Journal of Educational Technology, 21*, 82–101.

Graf, S. (2007). *Adaptivity in learning management systems focusing on learning styles*. Vienna: Vienna University of Technology.

Graf, S., & Kinshuk. (2006, July). *An approach for detecting learning styles in learning management systems* (pp. 161–163). Proceedings of the International Conference on Advances Learning Technologies (ICALT 06), Kerkrade.

Graf, S., & Kinshuk. (2007). Providing adaptive courses in learning management systems with respect to learning styles. In *Proceedings of the World Conference on E-Learning in Corporate, Government, Healthcare, and Higher Education (e-Learn)* (pp. 2576–2583). Chesapeake, VA: AACE Press.

Graf, S., Kinshuk, & Ives, C. (2010). A flexible mechanism for providing adaptivity based on learning styles in Learning Management Systems. In *Proceedings of the IEEE International Conference on Advanced Learning Technologies (ICALT)* (pp. 30–34). Sousse, Tunisia: IEEE Computer Society.

Graf, S., Lin, T., Jeffrey, L., & Kinshuk. (2006). An exploratory study of the relationship between learning styles and cognitive traits. *Proceedings of the European Conference on Technology Enhanced Learning (EC- 06)* (pp 470–475), Crete, Greece.

Graf, S., Lan, C. H., Liu, T. C., & Kinshuk. (2009). Investigations about the effects and effectiveness of adaptivity for students with different learning styles. In: *Proceedings of the IEEE international conference on advanced learning technologies (ICALT 2009)* (pp. 415–419). Los Alamitos, CA: IEEE Computer Society Press.

Gruber, T. (2008). Collective knowledge intelligence: where the social Web meets the semantic Web. *Web Semantics: Science, Services and Agents on the World Wide Web, 6,* 4–13.

Hargreaves, D. (2004). *Personalising learning: Next steps in working laterally.* London: Specialist Schools Trust.

Hase, S., & Kenyon, C. (2000). *From andragogy to heutagogy.* ultiBASE eJournal RMIT University.

Honey, P., & Mumford, A. (1982). *The manual of learning styles.* Maidenhead: Peter Honey.

Hopkins, D. (2007). *Every school a great school: Realizing the potential of system leadership.* Maidenhead: McGraw Hill.

Jonassen, D. H., & Land, S. M. (2000). *Theoretical foundations of learning environment.* Totowa, NJ: Lawrence Erlbaum Associates.

Joyce, B., Weil, M., & Calhoun, E. (2000). *Models of teaching* (6th ed.). Boston: Allyn & Bacon.

Karrer, T. (2008). Work learning - Same thing. *eLearning Technology.* Retrieved December 15, 2009 from http://elearningtech.blogspot.com/2008/02/pwle-not-ple-knowledge-work-not.html

Keller, F. S. (1968). Good-bye, teacher. *Journal of Applied Behaviour Analysis, 1,* 79–89.

Kern, R., Ware, P., & Warschauer, M. (2004). Crossing frontiers: New directions in online pedagogy and research. *Annual Review of Applied Linguistics, 24,* 243–60.

Kilpatrick, W. H. (1918). The project method. *Teachers College Record, 19,* 319–335.

Knowles, M. S. (1970). *The modern practice of adult education: Andragogy versus pedagogy.* New York: Associated Press.

Kolb, D. A. (1984). *Experiential learning: Experience as the source of learning and development.* Upper Saddle River, NJ: Prentice-Hall.

Kort, B., & Reilly, R. (2002). Theories for deep change in affect-sensitive cognitive machines: A constructivist model. *Educational Technology & Society 5(4).*

Kramer, J., Noronha, S., & Vergo, J. (2000). A user-centered design approach to personalization. *Communications of the ACM, 43,* 45–48.

Kuljis, J., & Liu, F. (2005). A comparison of learning style theories on the suitability for elearning. In M. H. Hamza (Ed.), *Proceedings of the IASTED Conference on Web Technologies, Applications, and Services* (pp. 191–197). Calgary, AB: ACTA Press.

Leadbeater, C. (2004). *Personalisation through participation: A new script for public services.* London: Demos.

Leadbeater, C. (2009). *We-think: Mass innovation, not mass production.* London: Profile Books.

LEADLAB. (2010). *European model of personalisation for adult learners.* European Grundtvig Project LEADLAB - Leading Elderly and Adult Development LAB (1.11.2009–31.10.2011). Retrieved September 3, 2011 from http://www.leadlab.euproject.org/go.cfm?PageId=6001

Leo, T., Manganello, F., & Chen, N.-S. (2010). From the learning work to the learning adventure. In *Proceedings of EDEN 2010 Annual Conference* (pp 9–11), Valencia, Spain.

Leone, S. (2009). *PLE: A brick in the construction of a lifelong learning society.* Technology Supported Environment for Personalised Learning Methods and Case Studies.

Leone, S. (2010, March). F2F learning vs. eLearning: The lifelong learner's point of view. *Proceedings of INTED 2010,* Valencia, Spain.

Leone, S., & Guazzaroni, G. (2010). *Pedagogical sustainability of interoperable formal and informal learning environments. Developing and utilizing e-learning applications.* Hershey, PA: IGI Global.

Levy, P. (1997). *Collective intelligence: Mankind's emerging world in cyberspace.* Cambridge: Perseus.

Limongelli, C., Sciarrone, F., Temperini, M., & Vaste, G. (2009). Adaptive learning with the LS-Plan system: A field evaluation. *IEEE Transactions on Learning Technologies, 2,* 203–215.

Limongelli, C., Sciarrone, F., & Vaste, G. (2011). Personalized e-learning in Moodle: The Moodle_LS system. *Journal of e-Learning and Knowledge Society, 7,* 49–58.

Littky, D., & Allen, F. (1999). Whole school personalization: One school at a time. *Educational Leadership, 57,* 2–6.

Litzinger, T. A., Lee, S. H., Wise, J. C., & Felder, R. M. (2007). A psychometric study of the index of learning styles. *Journal of Engineering Education, 96*, 309–319.

Lubesky, R. (2006). *The present and future of Personal Learning Environments (PLE)*. Optusnet.

Maharey, S. (2007). *Organising for personalising learning*. Wellington: Ministry of Education Media Release, New Zealand Government.

Martinez-Pons, M. (2002). A social cognitive view of parental influences on student academic self-regulation. *Theory into Practice, 41*, 126–131.

McAuliffe, M., Hargreaves, D., Winter, A., & Chadwick, G. (2009) Does pedagogy still rule? *Australasian Journal of Engineering Education, 15*(1).

McLoughlin, C., & Lee, M. J. W. (2010). Personalised and self regulated learning in the Web 2.0 era: International exemplars of innovative pedagogy using social software. *Australasian Journal of Educational Technology, 26*, 28–43.

Minocha, S. (2009). *A study on the effective use of social software by further and higher education in the UK to support student learning and engagement*. Bristol: JISC.

Monachesi, P., & Markus, F. T. (2010, May). Socially driven ontology enrichment for eLearning. *Proceedings of the Language Resources and Evaluation Conference*, Valletta, Malta.

Monachesi, P., Markus, F. T., Westerhout, E. N., Osenova, P., & Simov, K. (2011). Supporting formal and informal learning through domain ontologies. *e-Education, e-Business, e-Management, and e-Learning – IEEE, 2*(2), 117–121.

Motschnig-Pitrik, R., & Mallich, K. (2004). Effects of person-centered attitudes on professional and social competence in a blended learning paradigm. *Educational Technology & Society, 7*, 176–192.

National College. (2011). *About personalising learning*. Nottingham: National College.

New Media Consortium. (2009). The *Horizon report: 2009 edition*. Austin, TX: NMC.

O'Reilly, T. (2005). *What is Web 2.0 design patterns and business models for the next generation of software*. Retrieved September 18, 2007 from http://www.oreillynet.com/pub/a/oreilly/tim/news/2005/09/30/what-is-web-20.html?page=1

OCSE – Organisation for Economic Cooperation Development. (2006). *Schooling for tomorrow: Personalising education*. Paris: Centre for Educational Research and Innovation, OECD.

Oppermann, R. (1994). Introduction. In R. Oppermann (Ed.), *Adaptive user support: Ergonomic design of manually and automatically adaptable software* (pp. 1–13). Hillsdale, NJ: Lawrence Erlbaum Associates.

Oppermann, R., Rashev, R., & Kinshuk. (1997). Adaptability and adaptivity in learning systems. In *Proceedings of the International Conference on Knowledge Transfer* (pp. 173–179), Pace, London.

Oppermann, R., & Simm, H. (1994). Adaptability: User-initiated individualization. In R. Oppermann (Ed.), *Adaptive user support: Ergonomic design of manually and automatically adaptable software* (pp. 14–64). Hillsdale, NJ: Lawrence Erlbaum Associates.

Owen, M., Grant, L., Sayers, S., & Facer, K. (2006). *Social software and learning*. Bristol: Futurelab.

Parkhurst, H. (1922). *Education on the Dalton plan*. New York: E. P. Dutton.

Pask, G. (1976). Styles and strategies of learning. *British Journal of Educational Psychology, 46*, 128–148.

Pettenati, M. C. (2010). *Proposal of a personal knowledge environment*. Retrieved August 8, 2011 from http://knowbie.wordpress.com/tag/personal-knowledge-environment/

Popescu, E. (2008). *Dynamic adaptive hypermedia systems for e-learning*. Romania: Université de Craiova.

Posea, V., & Trausan-Matu, S. (2010). Bringing the social semantic Web to the personal learning environment. In *Proceedings of the 10th IEEE International Conference on Advanced Learning Technologies (ICALT)*. Sousse, Tunisia: IEEE Computer Society.

Rogers, C. R. (1983). *Freedom to learn for the 80's*. Columbus, OH: Charles E. Merrill.

Salaway, G., Caruso, J. B., & Nelson, M. R. (2008). *The ECAR study of undergraduate students and information technology 2008*. Boulder, CO: EDUCAUSE Center for Applied Research.

Sangineto, E., Capuano, N., Gaeta, M., & Micarelli, A. (2008). Adaptive course generation through learning styles representation. *Universal Access in the Information Society, 7*, 1–23.

Sclater, N. (2008). *Web 2.0, personal learning environments, and the future of learning management systems* (Research Bulletin, Issue 13). Boulder, CO: EDUCAUSE Center for Applied Research.

Seely-Brown, J. (1999). *Learning, working and playing in the digital age.* Retrieved June 15, 2009 from http://serendip.brynmawr.edu/sci_edu/seelybrown/

Seely-Brown, J. (2009). *Learning in the digital age.* Retrieved June 15, 2009 from http://www.johnseelybrown.com/

Siemens, G. (2004). Connectivism: A learning theory for the digital age. *International Journal of Instructional Technology and Distance Learning.* Retrieved August 8, 2011 from http://www.itdl.org/Journal/Jan_05/article01.htm

Siemens, G. (2006). Connectivism: *Learning Theory or Pastime of the Self-Amused?* Retrieved June, 6, 2011 from http://www.elearnspace.org/Articles/connectivism_self-amused.htm

Steeples, C., & Jones, C. (2002). *Networked learning: Perspectives and issues* (2nd ed.). Berlin: Springer.

Stubbé, H. E., & Theunissen, N. C. M. (2008). Self-directed adult learning in a ubiquitous learning environment: A meta-review. In: M. Kalz, R. Koper VH-P, & ML (ed) *Proceedings of the First Workshop on Technology Support for Self-Organized Learners* (pp. 5–28). Aachen: RWTH Aachen University.

Surowiecki, J. (2004). *The wisdom of crowds.* New York: Anchor Books.

Trentin, G. (2005). From "formal" to "informal" e-Learning through knowledge management and sharing. *Journal of e-Learning and Knowledge Society, 1,* 209–217.

Tseng, J. C. R., Chu, H.-C., Hwang, G.-J., & Tsai, C.-C. (2008). Development of an adaptive learning system with two sources of personalization information. *Computers & Education, 51,* 776–786.

UNESCO. (1999). *The world declaration on higher education for the twenty-first century: Vision and action.* Paris: UNESCO.

UNESCO Institute for Education (1999) Glossary of adult learning in Europe. UNESCO, Paris.

Varisco, B. M. (2002). *Costruttivismo socio-culturale Genesi filosofiche, sviluppi psico-pedagogici, applicazioni didattiche.* Roma: Carocci.

Via, W. (2010) *Personal learning networks for educators.* Retrieved May 17, 2011 from http://www.youtube.com/user/skipvia#p/a/u/1/q6WVEFE-oZA

Von Glasersfeld, E. (1998). *Il costruttivismo radicale. Una via per conoscere ed apprendere.* Roma: Società Stampa Sportiva.

Vygotsky, L. S. (1986). *Thought and language.* Cambridge, MA: MIT Press.

Washburne, C. (1941). *A living philosophy of education.* Chicago: The University of Chicago Press.

Westerhout, E. N., Monachesi, P., Markus, F. T., & Posea, V. (2010). Enhancing the learning process: Qualitative validation of an informal learning support system consisting of a knowledge discovery and a social learning component. In M. Wolpers, P. A. Kirschner, M. Scheffel, et al. (Eds.), *Sustaining TEL: From innovation to learning and practice* (Lecture Notes in Computer Science, Vol. 6383, pp. 374–389). Berlin: Springer.

Wheeler, S. (2011a). *Digital age learning.* Retrieved September 30, 2011 from http://steve-wheeler.blogspot.com/2011/07/digital-age-learning.html

Wheeler, S. (2011b). *Personalised learning.* Retrieved September 30, 2011 from http://steve-wheeler.blogspot.com/2010/11/personalised-learning.html

Wild, F., Modritscher, F., & Sigurdarson, S. (2008). *Designing for change: Mash-up personal learning environments.* eLearning Papers.

Winne, P. H. (1997). Experimenting to bootstrap self-regulated learning. *Journal of Educational Psychology, 89,* 397–410.

Zhou, L., Ding, L., & Finin, T. (2011). How is the semantic Web evolving? A dynamic social network perspective. *Computers in Human Behavior, 27*(4), 1294–1302.

Zimmerman, B. J. (1990). Self-regulated learning and academic achievement: An overview. *Educational Psychologist, 25,* 3–17.

Zimmerman, B. J. (2002). Becoming a self-regulated learner: An overview. *Theory into Practice, 41,* 64–72.

Chapter 2
The *SSW4LL* Format

Abstract This chapter develops the characterisation of a PLE as a LLL tool by detailing the *SSW4LL* (*Social Semantic Web for Lifelong Learners*) format. After an overview about the aims, possible scenarios and elements of the *SSW4LL* format, a motivated choice of adult lifelong learners' needs that *SSW4LL* aims to meet is developed. Subsequently, the chapter illustrates the learning paradigm and strategies that underpin *SSW4LL*. Then, the *SSW4LL system*, the technological architecture, is presented as a whole made up of components of formal and informal learning environments. The formal learning environment is devised by Moodle 2.0; a description and an evaluation of Moodle 2.0 features are provided, with a focus on the potential of its conditional activities as a suitable mechanism of learning adaptation. Concurrently, this part identifies the benefits of Felder–Silverman's learning style model, which was selected as the most suitable learning style model for the use in LMSs. The elements of the informal learning environment, Semantic MediaWiki, Diigo and Google+, are presented and their implications within the *SSW4LL* format are discussed. The next section of the chapter deals with the organisation of the format: the resources needed a user case scenario, and a flow chart of the steps of the format implementation are outlined. Finally, a SWOT analysis provides evaluation elements for the format.

2.1 Overview

The *SSW4LL* format aims to provide a learner-centred framework to support the characterisation of adult lifelong learners' PLEs through implicit and explicit tools of personalisation. The format is suitable for adult lifelong learners in general, rather than for one specific target within, and for the development of all knowledge domains. Further, the *SSW4LL* format supports mobile learning, but ubiquitous learning features (Leone & Leo, 2011) could be implemented as well, as an extension.

S. Leone, *Characterisation of a Personal Learning Environment as a Lifelong Learning Tool*, SpringerBriefs in Education, DOI 10.1007/978-1-4614-6274-3_2,
© Springer Science+Business Media New York 2013

The synergy of formal and informal learning is realised through the smooth integration of the different technological components, the light e-moderation of the learning environment by a facilitator, the support of a technical e-tutor and the continuous enrichment of the initial learning resources (formal environment) by social software and Social Semantic Web tools (informal environment).

The *SSW4LL* system, the technological architecture, is made up of Moodle 2.0 integrated with an adaptive mechanism (conditional activities), as the formal learning environment component, and of Semantic MediaWiki, Diigo and Google+, as Social Semantic Web tools and informal learning environment elements.

As a whole, the *SSW4LL* format offers an adaptive (Oppermann & Simm, 1994) modular, flexible and integrated architecture, compatible with future Moodle releases.

2.2 Needs Analysis

In relation to the European reference framework of key competences for LLL (European Parliament and Council of the European Union, 2006) and to the results of the EU survey on adult education (AES) (European Commission, 2011),[1] the *SSW4LL* format can contribute to:

1. learning to learn;
2. form active citizens, that is individuals who are engaged in the development of the multiple dimensions of citizenship, beyond knowledge towards the enhancement of competences and attitudes by experiencing active participation in different contexts;
3. personalised and flexible learning;
4. facilitate learner-centred technology-enhanced learning;
5. promote inclusion;
6. improve digital skills;
7. improve social skills.

2.3 Learning Paradigm and Strategies

The *SSW4LL* format is devised to personalise learning in terms of self-organisation by adult lifelong learners working with the support provided by the facilitator, the adaptive mechanism, the technical e-tutor and the peers (Leadbeater, 2004). In this format, personalisation aims to valorise learners' full potential and to empower individuals through knowledge sharing and co-construction. Learners are active co-designers of the learning experience (Maharey, 2007). Consequently, rather than consisting in *learning work*, learning becomes a *learning adventure* (Leo, Manganello, & Chen, 2010), that is a learner-centred, holistic experience which involves a complex, continual, chaotic and co-creative process.

---

[1] See Sect. 1.1.

The format is developed on the background of andragogy (Knowles, 1970) and socio-constructivism (Varisco, 2002; Vygotsky, 1986) theories. Learning is negotiated between the facilitator, the learners and the learning material, and expertise can be located beyond the formal setting through learners' PLEs (Drexler, 2010). In this way, networked learning opens to peer-to-peer scaffolding (Bruner, 1960; Corneli & Danoff, 2011), is made possible by social software, is process-based, experiential (Kolb, 1984), anchored in and driven by learners' interests and, as a result, promotes self-regulated, independent learning (Zimmerman, 1990). Learners enter the learning path with a great diversity of experience, are life-centred, task-centred or problem-centred, and are motivated by internal self-esteem, recognition, better quality of life and self-actualisation (Knowles, 1970).

Herein, a PLE is a concept that helps to view the subject as a landscape as well as individual pieces of information. A PLE consists in a group of techniques and a variety of tools to gather information, explore and develop relationships between pieces of information, to communicate and collaborate (Leone & Guazzaroni, 2010). Information and knowledge reside in digital sources (locally produced files and notes, Internet/Intranet, e-learning courses, reference sites, text/audio/video/graphics files, shared presentations, RSS feeds) and in non-digital sources (books and journals, classroom-based courses, professional meetings, live interaction with colleagues, friends and family). A PLE, at the same time, develops and is fed by autonomy, pragmatic, relevance, building on prior knowledge, goal-directed approach (Leone, 2009).

2.3.1 Learning Strategies

The *SSW4LL* format can be developed through the following strategies:

- brainstorming (in Moodle forums, and in Google+ by posts, huddles and video hangouts);
- problem solving;
- collaborative and cooperative learning (in Moodle forums, Diigo and Semantic MediaWiki);
- webquest (which includes cooperative work and problem solving);
- reflection activities;
- learning by doing;
- self-learning, with the support of an adaptive mechanism in the formal learning environment (Moodle).

2.3.2 Evaluation and Assessment

The *SSW4LL* format is monitored through an entry and a final survey, and entry and formative self-assessment tests to evaluate its effectiveness in terms of participants' expectations and satisfaction and achievement of learning goals, respectively. A final cooperative essay or project work provides summative assessment.

2.4   Technological Architecture: The *SSW4LL* System

The *SSW4LL* system is the technological architecture of the *SSW4LL* format. This system is made up of integrated components of formal and informal learning environments. The system has been designed, implemented and successfully validated as a device suitable to provide adult lifelong learners with a dynamically personalised learning environment, and with a sense of ownership and control over their own learning and career planning.

In particular, the design of the framework has been developed considering (Giovannella, 2008):

- the Web used as an environment, where various tools and contents can be aggregated for the construction of a PLE;
- open source, open content, open society and, as a result, adoption of open "machine-readable" standards;
- the learner's capability of managing his/her learning processes and of configurating his/her e-portfolio as aggregator of personal knowledge and competences (Lubesky, 2006).

In the *SSW4LL* system the formal learning environment is devised by Moodle 2.0, in which adaptive learning is enabled by its conditional activities. The elements of the informal learning environment are Semantic MediaWiki, Diigo and Google+ that allow adult lifelong learners for a qualitative different bottom-up approach to learning (Fig. 2.1).

By fully exploiting Moodle 2.0 adaptation features that in the *SSW4LL* system are based on the detection of learners' learning styles, this LMS can deploy a personalised scaffolded learning environment for self-regulated learners. Further, social software can be smoothly integrated in the architecture by widgets and by allowing login sessions to never expire.

In the following, a description and an evaluation of Moodle 2.0 features are provided, with a focus on the potential of its conditional activities as a suitable mechanism of learning adaptation. Concurrently, this part identifies the benefits of FSLSM, which was selected as the most suitable learning style model for the use in LMSs. Finally, the elements of the informal learning environment (Semantic MediaWiki, Diigo and Google+) are presented, and their implications within the *SSW4LL* format are discussed.

2.4.1   *Formal Learning Environment: Moodle 2.0*

All LMSs provide a great variety of features that teachers can exploit to create and deliver online courses (e.g. learning resources, quizzes, forums, wikis, chats, etc.). For this reason, they are commonly used by educational institutions to successfully offer technology-enhanced learning. Nevertheless, LMSs typically do not consider the individual differences of learners and provide very little or, in most cases, no adaptivity (Graf, 2007).

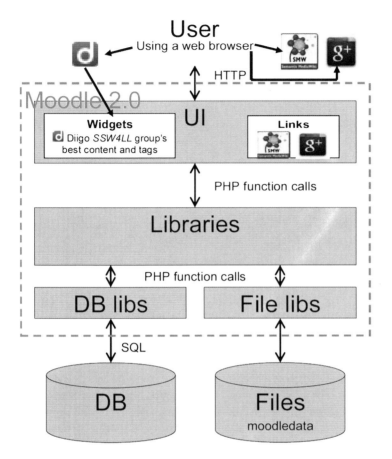

Fig. 2.1 The *SSW4LL* system architecture

Further, the knowledge society and the current LLL vision have urged a wide range of skills to be developed in lifelong learners: the ability to locate and evaluate information effectively and efficiently; facility with making meaning by aligning new information with prior knowledge and an ability to synthesise, critically analyse and create new information within the context of larger social practices (Lin, 2011).

Starting from these preliminary remarks, two relevant studies and prior direct experience of the author of this research have supported the choice of Moodle 2.0 as the most suitable component for the formal learning environment in the *SSW4LL* system.

The first reference is Graf's (2007) evaluation of 36 open source LMSs, aiming at assessing the general functionality and usage of LMSs, and their ability to be extended to provide adaptive courses on the basis of students' learning styles.

In a pre-evaluation phase, Graf defined three minimum criteria concerning the usage of LMSs: an active community, a stable development status and a good documentation of the system. An active community shows that the system is supported and used by many other people, who can provide help in case of need. Thus, an active community indirectly indicates a good quality of the system. A stable development status indicates a reliable and not error-prone product, which is executable in an operational environment. The availability of good documentation is crucial for the installation and customisation of the system, and avoids nearly exclusive dependence on the LMS community. As a forth parameter, Graf considered the focus of the system on the presentation of content as the minimum criterion related to the teaching objectives of the LMS.

Nine LMSs out of the initial 36 met all four criteria, and they were tested in detail through an example course. Finally, to evaluate the nine LMSs, their characteristics were divided into eight categories (communication tools, learning objects, management of user data, usability, adaptation, technical aspects, administration, course management) and several subcategories, which were then weighted and assessed, based on the experience from the usage of each LMS when conducting the example course.

The results of Graf's evaluation highlight that Moodle achieves the best ratings with respect to overall functionality and usage, and adaptation aspects.

Although this evaluation was conducted in 2005,[2] and many new versions of the investigated LMSs were released in the meantime, Moodle can still be seen as one of the leading LMSs.

Currently, Moodle is one of the most widely used LMSs in the world, by over 31 million students in over 44 thousand sites in over 200 countries (Cooch, 2010), and many universities switched to it as their official LMS in the last few years. Moreover, a second relevant and recent study confirms the validity of Moodle in its new version.[3] As a matter of fact, Lin (2011) evaluated the potential of Moodle 2.0 for helping lifelong learners master the wide range of skills and competences that the twenty-first century requires. Lin examined Moodle 2.0 using the following guiding criteria (Cummins et al., 2007) (corresponding features of the LMS are provided in brackets):

1. providing cognitive challenges and opportunities for deep processing of meaning (e.g. by the glossary, forum and quiz modules);
2. relating instruction to prior knowledge and experiences (by the mindmap and questionnaire modules to activate brainstorming and connections);
3. promoting active self-regulated collaborative inquiry (collaboration and social interaction can be embedded in almost every module and block via chat, forum and the improved wiki);
4. encouraging extensive involvement in all language skills (by the RSS feeds block to link authentic reading materials from external websites; by the new repository to easily integrate authentic resources from YouTube and Flickr; by the personal profile and the assignment, lesson, journal, blog and forum modules to develop writing skills);

---

[2] Graf evaluated Moodle 1.4.1 version.

[3] Moodle 2.0 was released at the end of 2010.

5. developing multiple strategies for effective language learning (by the page layout to let students track important information, by the new *My private files* to arrange materials, by built-in comment boxes and the new workshop module);
6. promoting identity investment (by tools available in several blocks and by *My Moodle* page).

As a whole, Lin's review is extremely positive. In the author's view, Moodle 2.0 is a powerful software package whose primary strengths lie in its technical features and in the learning approach that underpins it. Moodle 2.0 enables educational designers to create flexible learning environments based on their students' perceived needs, intentions, cognitive traits and learning strategies. Moodle 2.0 allows facilitators to enhance meaningful learning environments and support lifelong learners in being successful.

Finally, the numerous direct experiences of the author of this research, as a lifelong learner, and as an educational designer and a teacher–facilitator, particularly for adult lifelong learners, strongly confirm the advantages of adopting Moodle as an LMS, and Moodle 2.0 in particular.

In brief, the elements that have supported the choice of Moodle 2.0 as the most suitable component for the formal learning environment in the *SSW4LL* system are:

1. it is an open source and flexible LMS;
2. it is supported and constantly improved by an active community;
3. in comparison with its previous versions, Moodle 2.0 offers a new way of managing content (media from sites like Youtube and Flickr can be easily embedded from the text editor), some existing activities updated and improved (e.g. wiki, workshop and quiz), a flexible mechanism to personalise, check and scaffold learners' progress (conditional activities) and improved administration (e.g. a clearer attribution of roles by *cohorts*).

Since Moodle's design and development draws upon social constructionist philosophy,[4] it is devised particularly for teachers who facilitate their students' learning, rather than lecture to them; for learners to be in charge of their own learning, discussing, collaborating and actively *constructing* their own knowledge; for learners to find their own path, rather than to follow a path set down for them by someone else. Nevertheless, Moodle 2.0 also allows the implementation of different degrees of learning personalisation between the following extremes (a) teachers can choose to roughly guide students, by scaffolding, and let them find their own way; (b) teachers can choose to give them a detailed map with checkpoints they must reach along the way, that is a more structured approach. Further, the determination of learners' learning styles is possible by creating a suitable quiz.[5]

In the *SSW4LL* format, the above-mentioned option (a) and the FSLSM (Felder & Silverman, 1988) are adopted to meet learners' needs and profiles, in accordance with the theoretical background of the format. Furthermore, several researchers

---

[4] http://docs.moodle.org/en/Philosophy.

[5] For Moodle 1.9 a special plug-in can be added http://moodle.org/mod/forum/discuss.php?d=140054.

concur on the validity of the FSLSM as the most appropriate to be used in adaptive learning systems (Carver, Howard, & Lane, 1999; Graf, Kinshuk, & Ives, 2010; Kuljis & Liu, 2005; Limongelli, Sciarrone, & Vaste, 2011), as the *SSW4LL* system is.

Specifically, the FSLSM describes a learner's learning style in very much detail, assuming that each learner has a preference on each of the four dimensions (1) active/reflective, (2) sensing/intuitive, (3) visual/verbal and (4) sequential/global, with assignable values on a −11 to +11 scale. Felder and Spurlin (2005) summarise the four dimensions as follows:

- *active* (learn by trying things out, enjoy working in groups) or *reflective* (learn by thinking things through, prefer working alone or with one or two familiar partners);
- *sensing* (concrete, practical, oriented towards facts and procedures) or *intuitive* (conceptual, innovative, oriented towards theories and underlying meanings);
- *visual* (prefer visual representations of presented material, such as pictures, diagrams and flow charts) or *verbal* (prefer written and spoken explanations);
- *sequential* (linear thinking process, learn in incremental steps) or *global* (holistic thinking process, learn in large leaps).

By using dimensions, instead of types, and a numerical evaluation, the strengths of students' preference for a determined learning style can be evidenced; besides, the FSLSM is based on tendencies, and thus allows to consider exceptional behaviour.

In the *SSW4LL* format, the 44-question *Index of Learning Styles Questionnaire* (ILS) (Felder & Soloman, 1997)[6] is adapted into a quiz of four questions, that is one for each of the four dimensions of the FSLSM; each question allows learners to answer by choosing an option between the two provided by a drop-down menu and by attributing a value between 0 and 11 to that option (Fig. 2.2).[7] A short description of the options is given to support learners' choice.

Even if the original ILS is shortened to facilitate students, its dichotomous structure is kept to force a decision between the two alternatives, thereby increasing the chances that the instrument response will detect preferences.

The feedback provided to the students is a short description of their resulting learning style. In all, 16 different learning profiles have been written as combinations of the eight style categories within the ILS, two for each of the four dimensions. In the back end, the correct matching of the options that learners indicate for each dimension with the final learning profile requires the educational designer to be very familiar with Moodle 2.0 question templates and quiz settings.

The detection of learners' learning profiles is the starter of personalised learning sequences by fully exploiting Moodle 2.0 conditional activities[8] and the *activity completion tracking* facility (Cooch, 2010).

---

[6] Available at http://www.engr.ncsu.edu/learningstyles/ilsweb.html.

[7] This question format is obtained by integrating a Moodle template of a true–false question with the necessary HTML code.

[8] A workaround to controlling students' access was made available for Moodle 1.9: *activity locking* was a means whereby a teacher could set certain conditions on a task that a learner had to meet before the next task became visible. With Moodle 2.0 this feature is standard, by conditional activities (Cooch, 2010).

Fig. 2.2 The quiz for the detection of learning styles in the *SSW4LL* format

2.4.1.1 Adaptation Model

In the *SSW4LL* format, conditional activities aim to allow the educational designer to scaffold learners in accessing learning resources on the basis of one or more conditions. As Fig. 2.3 shows, in the back end of the resources and activities (e.g. a forum) that the designer previously wishes to add to the course, a *restrict availability* area is available for setting. The resource availability can be enabled on a date, on a certain grade for a determined activity or for more than one, on the

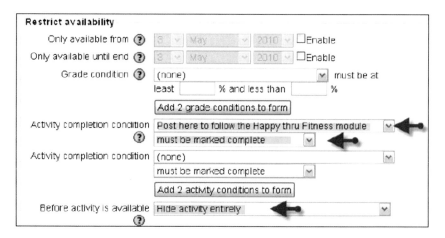

Fig. 2.3 An example of the setting of conditional activities

completion of a determined activity or for more than one. If all these options are set, they have to be met all together to allow learners to visualise and access this activity (i.e. the forum).

The second element to make the learning environment adaptive is the *activity completion tracking* facility, which is the ability for users to mark tasks as "done". Next to each item on the Moodle course page, a dotted check mark (tick) can be either manually checked by the students, if they feel they have finished a task (they can change their mind), or else the teacher can set it to be checked automatically once the student has actually completed the activity.

In the *SSW4LL* format a suitable and thorough combination of these conditions lets create different learning sequences, in which LOs are proposed according to the students' learning profiles that are initially detected through the quiz (Table 2.1).

In order to choose the most suitable kinds of LOs for the *SSW4LL* format, the type of learning resources of several e-learning environments for adult learners have been analysed:

1. Graf et al.'s (2010) model: in a teacher-centred (but constructivist in its aims) learning environment for ICT undergraduates, delivered in Moodle 1.9 integrated with an adaptive mechanism based on learning styles, 12 structured kinds of LOs are provided accordingly. Video/audio LOs are not considered.
2. Ghislandi's model (Leone & Guazzaroni, 2010): in a moderately teacher-centred (but socio-constructivist in its aims) learning environment for PhD students, delivered in Moodle 1.9, a few kinds of textual LOs are scheduled. No strategy nor tools for personalising learning have been adopted.

Table 2.1 *SSW4LL* LOs sequencing according to the different learning styles

Dimensions	Learning styles	Learners' features	LOs in *SSW4LL*
1	Active	They prefer to learn by trying things out and discussing with others about the learned material.	1. Commentary 2. Animation 3. Real-life application 4. Reading 5. Self-assessment test 6. Forum activity 7. Reflection quiz
	Reflective	They learn by thinking and reflecting about the material; prefer to read the content first.	1. Commentary 2. Reading 3. Reflection quiz 4. Real-life application 5. Self-assessment test 6. Animation
2	Sensing	They prefer concrete material, are more practical oriented, and like to relate the learned material to the real world; tend to be patient with details and like standard procedures as well as practical problem solving.	1. Commentary 2. Animation 3. Real-life application 4. Reading 5. Self-assessment test
	Intuitive	They like abstract materials such as concepts and theories, prefer open-ended questions, tend to be more creative and like challenges.	1. Commentary 2. Reading 3. Reflection quiz 4. Animation 5. Real-life application 6. Forum activity
3	Visual	They remember best what they see—pictures, diagrams, flow charts, time lines, demonstrations and films. Everyone learns more when information is presented both visually and verbally.	1. Commentary 2. Animations 3. Reading 4. Real-life application 5. Self-assessment test 6. Forum activity
	Verbal	They get more out of words—written and spoken explanations. Everyone learns more when information is presented both visually and verbally.	1. Commentary 2. Reading 3. Forum activity 4. Real-life application 5. Self-assessment test 6. Animation
4	Sequential	They expect guidance and a linear increase of complexity in learning; they tend to be good in using and applying partial knowledge.	1. Commentary 2. Reading 3. Reflection quiz 4. Self-assessment test 5. Animation 6. Real-life application 7. Forum activity
	Global	They get the big picture of the topic and learn in large jumps, almost randomly; they may be able to solve complex problems quickly or put things together in novel ways once they have grasped the big picture, but they may have difficulty explaining how they did it.	1. Commentary 2. Real-life application 3. Reading 4. Animation 5. Reflection quiz 6. Self-assessment test 7. Forum activity

3. SLOOP2desc[9] model (Fulantelli & Oprea, 2011): in a moderately teacher-centred, strongly hands-on learning environment for high-school teachers and educational designers, delivered in Moodle 1.9, four kinds of LOs are provided, most of which in video. No strategy nor tools for personalising learning have been adopted.
4. Technology Enhanced Knowledge Research Institute (TEKRI) at Athabasca University's PLENK2010[10] model: in a learner-centred, connectivist learning environment, learning resources are unstructured, open and distributed over multiple systems. Learners personalise their learning independently.
5. University of Illinois Springfield's eduMOOC2010[11] model: it devises a way to connect and collaborate engaging in the learning process, in which learning resources are unstructured, open and distributed over multiple systems. A distributed knowledge base is built on a LLL background, and learners personalise their learning independently.
6. Limongelli et al.'s (2011) model: in a quite learner-centred learning environment for adult lifelong learners, delivered in Moodle 1.9 integrated with the adaptive plug-in LS-Plan based on learning styles and prior knowledge, only a few kinds of textual LOs are scheduled.

The evaluation of these models has been carried out considering their theoretical approach and the relevance and consistency of the scheme of resources. As a result, the following seven kinds of LOs have been identified for the *SSW4LL* format:

1. *Commentary* provides learners with a brief overview of the week/module and of the learning material proposed within.
2. *Readings* include Wikipedia items, proceedings, papers, white papers, book chapters, project deliverables about the content of a week/module.
3. *Animations* demonstrate the concepts of the course in an animated multimedia format (videos and ppt).
4. *Real-Life Applications* demonstrate how the learned material can be related to and applied in real-life situations (ongoing and recent projects).
5. *Reflection Quizzes* include one or more open-ended questions about the content of a week/module. The questions aim at encouraging learners to reflect about the learned material.

---

[9] *Sharing Learning Objects in an Open Perspective to Develop European Skills and Competences* (2010) http://www.sloop2desc.eu/en.html.

[10] *Personal Learning Environments Networks and Knowledge* http://connect.downes.ca/index.html.

[11] Edu *Massive Open Online Course* https://sites.google.com/site/edumooc/home.

6. *Forum Activities* provide learners with the possibility to ask questions and discuss topics with their peers and facilitator. While a course typically includes only one or few discussion forums, a course developed on the *SSW4LL* format can include several discussion forum activities as LOs that encourage learners to use the discussion forum.

7. *Self-Assessment Tests* include several close-ended questions about the content of a week/module. These questions allow learners to check their acquired knowledge and how well they know the content of the section already through receiving immediate feedback about their answers.

The seven LOs are differently sequenced according to the learning styles features (Table 2.1) and subsequently to the 16 learning profiles resulting from the combination of the eight style categories.

2.4.2   Informal Learning Environment: Semantic MediaWiki, Diigo and Google+

In the *SSW4LL* system the elements of the informal learning environment are Semantic MediaWiki, Diigo and Google+,

They have been selected among several alternative solutions on the basis of effectiveness and efficiency in relation to *SSW4LL* target learners' goals. In detail, evaluation has been conducted on the following criteria, attributing a value on a 5-point Likert scale (1 = strongly disagree, 2 = disagree, 3 = neutral, 4 = agree and 5 = strongly agree): social semantic features, effectiveness as tools for characterising adult lifelong learners' PLEs, novel features, possible integration with Moodle 2.0, easy-to-use interface and mobile learning features (Table 2.2).

The categories of tools that needed to be considered for the *SSW4LL* system were aggregators, tools of semantic annotation, social bookmarking and recommended search and social networks. Accordingly, after an initial analysis of a large number of applications, the following nine have been sieved and compared within their categories:

- as aggregators, Evri, Google Reader and Google+;
- as semantic annotation tools, Formal Learning Support System (FLSS) and Semantic MediaWiki;
- as social bookmarking tools, Google Reader and Diigo;
- as recommended search tools, Informal Learning Support System (iFLSS), Binocs and Google+;
- as social network, Google+.

Table 2.2 Comparative evaluation of the tools considered for the informal learning environment

Criteria/ Tools	Social semantic features					Characterisation of PLEs					Novel features					Integratable with Moodle 2.0					Easy-to-use interface					Mobile learning features					Value
	1	2	3	4	5	1	2	3	4	5	1	2	3	4	5	1	2	3	4	5	1	2	3	4	5	1	2	3	4	5	
Evri				x					x						x		x							x						x	26
FLSS			x					x						x		x							x						x		14
iFLSS					x				x				x			x							x							x	18
Binocs					x				x				x			x								x						x	21
Google Docs	x								x					x				x							x					x	25
Google Reader	x								x					x				x							x			x			26
Semantic MediaWiki			x					x						x			x					x						x			20
Diigo			x							x					x					x					x					x	29
Google+					x					x					x			x				x								x	29

In the following the characteristics of the elements assessed are presented, and the results of the evaluation and the implications of Semantic MediaWiki, Diigo and Google+ within the *SSW4LL* format are discussed.

Evri[12] is a free aggregator that automatically and constantly indexes millions of topic-specific streams from thousands of different sources to filter through the noise of the Web and deliver customised news. Evri's topic-based approach to news aggregation is a divergence from the older source-based paradigm. Its core technology platform relies on natural language processing and semantic search to deliver channels of aggregated content on millions of topics. It reconciles content against semi-structured and trend databases to determine result ranking.

The FLSS (Formal Learning Support System)[13] offers access to learning materials via semantic search techniques. A simple text search returns documents with a varying degree of relevance, by using different wordings of a concept and exploiting implicit semantic relations in the text. The system data include a domain ontology to provide a formal conceptualisation of a domain and semantically annotated LOs. The services provide search, edit and visualisation facilities to help the user access and modify the information; the user can also leave comments and remarks.

Nevertheless, validation reports emphasise that some requirements still lack for the smooth adoption of FLSS, among which exhaustive guidelines and use cases are crucial.

The iFLSS (Informal Learning Support System) consists of a range of services that support knowledge retrieval from Delicious, YouTube, Bibsonomy and Slideshare through a domain ontology enhanced with folksonomy and by recommending material on the basis of the content, tags and users belonging to the relevant social network (Monachesi & Markus, 2010; Monachesi, Markus, Westerhout, Osenova, & Simov, 2011). The widget-based visualisation of the system has a strong focus towards using an expert validated ontology for providing a structured overview of the domain, while social media services allow for personalisation of content recommendation (Posea & Trausan-Matu, 2010). Communication is facilitated

---

[12] http://www.evri.com.

[13] See Sect. 1.3.5 for an in-depth analysis of the LTfLL project and of FLSS and iFLSS.

through the use of social networks, and new communities of learners can be established through the recommendations provided by the system. However, since validation was aimed at an academic institution with a fixed curriculum, while the software was designed for a self-directed LLL context, an additional validation activity should be conducted on this target. Besides, a less elaborate method for setting up the system and an installation guide needs to be provided (Westerhout, Monachesi, Markus, & Posea, 2010).

Binocs[14] is a social search widget that searches over multiple databases (e.g. Youtube, Slideshare, etc.). It employs a federated search engine that aggregates heterogeneous resources and forwards them to a recommender system. Recommended resources ranging from wiki pages, videos, to presentations can be saved, shared, assessed and re-purposed according to each user's interest. To rank resources, the recommender system considers the following user's actions (1) selecting a resource from a search result, (2) liking or disliking a search result (using a thumbs up and down feature) and (3) previewing a search result. The recommender system relies on an algorithm influenced by Google's original PageRank algorithm (Page, Brin, Motwani, & Winograd, 1999) and based on the 3A interaction model (El Helou, Salzmann, & Gillet, 2010). In the absence of previous user interaction with a resource, ranking is still possible based on the resource relevance to the search query.

A preliminary evaluation of the widget's usability and recommendation usefulness helped to improve the user interface, and showed that, since users prefer Google results due to their diversity, more repositories should be added to the federated search engine. On the other hand, pilot users agreed on the usefulness of the collaborative recommendations on top of the search results (Modritscher et al., 2011).

Google Docs[15] is a free cloud computing document-sharing services. In comparison with other similar tools, its added value stands in its enhanced sharing features and accessibility. This Google's "software as a service" office suite allows to create, edit and share documents in real time among multiple users. Documents, spreadsheets, presentations can be created, imported through the Web interface or sent via email. Documents can be saved to a user's local computer in a variety of formats (ODF, HTML, PDF, RTF, Text, Microsoft Office), are automatically saved to Google's servers to prevent data loss and a revision history is automatically kept. Moreover, documents can be tagged and archived for organisational purposes. Users cannot be notified of changes, not even in real-time work, but users can see where in the document a particular editor is currently writing by an editor-specific colour/ cursor. Also, the revision history allows users to see the changes made to a document, distinguished by editor/colour. Besides, the application can notify users when a comment or discussion is made or replied to, facilitating collaboration.

---

[14] Binocs is developed in the context of the ROLE project. See Sect. 1.3.5.

[15] See an overview of Google Docs.

Google Reader[16] is a Web-based aggregator, capable of reading Atom and RSS feeds online or offline. As of 2010 its features include a front page that shows new items at a glance, import and export subscription lists as an OPML file, keyboard short-cuts for main functions, choice between *list view* or *expanded view* for item viewing, automatic marking of items as read as they are scrolled past and search in all feeds, across all updates from subscriptions. Part of the visual redesign of all Google products in 2011, a new Google Reader interface was available on October 31, 2011. Beside the sweeping visual changes, former social features ("share" and "like" buttons) have been removed and replaced by Google+'s "+1" button and the "share on Google+" box.

Semantic MediaWiki[17] is one of the most popular semantically enhanced collab-orative knowledge management systems, mostly because it aims to make semantic technologies accessible to non-expert users. Semantic MediaWiki is an extension to MediaWiki that enables users to semantically annotate wiki pages, based on which the wiki contents can be browsed, searched and reused in novel ways (Krötzsch, Vrandecic, Völkel, Haller, Studer, et al., 2007).

RDF and OWL are used in the background to formally annotate information in wiki pages. Every page corresponds to an ontological element (including classes and prop-erties) that might be further described by annotations on that same page, to allow users to understand where the information originated from and make maintenance easy.

Different namespaces are used to distinguish the semantic function of wiki pages. The namespaces are defined through the wiki configuration and cannot be defined by users. They can be individual elements (most of the pages, describing elements of the domain of interest), categories (to classify individual elements and to create subcategories), properties (relationships between two pages or a page and a data value) and types (to distinguish different kinds of properties).

Most annotations can easily be exported in terms of OWL DL: normal pages cor-respond to abstract individuals, properties correspond to OWL properties, categories correspond to OWL classes and property values can be abstract individuals or typed literals. Thus, most annotations are directly mapped to simple OWL statements, simi-lar to RDF triples (Bratsas, Kapsas, Konstantinidis, Koutsouridis, & Bamidis, 2009).

Templates and forms allow to restrict the user to a predefined set of annotations. The advantage of this mixture of guided input and open annotations is that the struc-ture of the data can evolve dynamically.

Although the usefulness of Semantic MediaWiki features attracts many potential users, issues about Semantic MediaWiki's resource requirements, stability and scalability are raised (Herzig & Ell, 2010).

Diigo[18] is two services in one: it is a research and collaborative research tool on the one hand and a knowledge-sharing community and social content site on the other. It provides a browser add-on that improves research productivity. Beyond bookmarking, Diigo allows to highlight portions of Web pages that are of particular

---

[16] See http://googlereader.blogspot.com/.

[17] http://semantic-mediawiki.org/wiki/Semantic_MediaWiki.

[18] http://www.diigo.com. Diigo is an acronym from "Digest of Internet Information, Groups and Other stuff".

interest to the user, and to attach sticky notes to specific parts of Web pages. Further, unlike most similar tools, Diigo highlights and sticky notes are persistent. Moreover, all the information are saved on Diigo servers, creating a user's personal digest of the Web that he/she can easily search, access, sort and share from any PC or even iPhone. Groups can be created.

Every Diigo user's tags and annotations feed a collectively enriched repository of content. Users can subscribe to any bookmark under any set of tags, and the system provides recommended news and resources personalised to their interests. Besides, while the user is on a Web page, the Diigo sidebar shows who else has bookmarked this page or this site, and what other similar pages and sites they have bookmarked, providing a social browsing experience and an efficient way to find related content and people. Subsequently, a user can connect with them in multiple ways: by inviting them to add him/her as a friend, sending them messages, inviting them to a group or simply adding them to her/his watch-list.

Google+ is a brand-new sharing network that lets users share different things with different people. Google+ main features are:

- *circles* that enable a user to organise contacts into groups for sharing across various Google products and services. Although other users can view the list of people in a user's collection of circles, they cannot view the names of those circles. Organisation is done through a drag-and-drop interface;
- *sparks* is a front-end to Google Search, enabling users to identify topics they might be interested in sharing with others. *Featured interests* Sparks are also available, based on topics others globally are finding interesting;
- *hangouts* are group video chat (with a maximum of 10 people participating in a single *Hangout*). However, anyone on the Web could potentially join in if they happen to possess the unique URL of the Hangout;
- *huddle* is a group messaging feature available within the Google+ mobile app. Rather than sending text messages to each person in a circle, the user sends *Huddle messages* to the group;
- the *+1* button lets users publicly recommend pages across the Web, share with the right circles on Google+, help improve Google Search as well, since Google shows which pages a user's social connections have +1'd right beneath search results and ads.

A core element of Google+ is its privacy features, which have been integrated deeply into the product. Google+ gives users extensive control over these features.

Table 2.2 shows the comparison between the nine applications against the six parameters relevant to the effectiveness and efficiency of the *SSW4LL* format. Discrete and total values highlight that Semantic MediaWiki, Diigo and Google+ are the best solutions to be integrated in the format. Within the different categories considered, values are:

- as aggregators, Evri = 26, Google Reader = 26 and Google+ = 29;
- as semantic annotation tools, FLSS = 14 and Semantic MediaWiki = 20;
- as social bookmarking tools, Google Reader = 26 and Diigo = 29;
- as recommended search tools, iFLSS = 18, Binocs = 21 and Google+ = 29;

- as social network, Google+ is the only solution considered in this final screening because it had already appeared as the most complete and innovative.

Semantic MediaWiki results slightly critical in its interface and in relation to mobile learning; however, it still is more flexible, collaborative, tested and documented than FLSS.

Google+, beyond being chosen for its characteristics as a social network, offers all together the features that Evri, iFLSS and Binocs provide. Further, iFLSS and Binocs cannot be integrated with Moodle 2.0. Besides, the validation of iFLSS is incomplete, the method of its setting is elaborate and no installation guide is provided. Finally, the validation test of Binocs showed that pilot users preferred Google results due to their diversity.

Diigo is decisively superior to Google Reader in relation to social semantic features, easy-to-use interface and integration with Moodle 2.0.

As a whole, the influence of the informal learning components of the *SSW4LL* system is strong. As a matter of fact, since a flexible and personalised learning environment requires that content can be accessed, evaluated, organised and reused with ease by the students, social software and Semantic Web technology play an important role in such learning environments. Where social software gives users freedom to choose their own processes and supports the collaboration of people *anytime, anywhere,* Semantic Web technology gives the possibility to structure information for easy retrieval, reuse and exchange between different systems and tools (Bratsas et al., 2009).

2.5 Organisation

2.5.1 *Technical Competences Required*

The implementation and management of the *SSW4LL* format requires various kinds and degrees of skills and knowledge. The professional profiles involved are a learning technologist, an ICT technician and a (or more) teacher–facilitator. The learning technologist's and the ICT technician's tasks could be accomplished by one professional with competences for both profiles.

The learning technologist has extensive knowledge of the use of Moodle, Semantic MediaWiki, Diigo and Google+, and of all the other technologies that could support learning and teaching within the *SSW4LL* format. He/she deals with the implementation, updating and troubleshooting of the different technological components of the format.

The ICT technician has knowledge of a range of ICT hardware and applications commonly used, and has good problem-solving and organisational skills. He/she provides the facilitator and learners with technical support, guidance and maintenance in order to use all software/hardware correctly during the learning path. He/she conveys technical tasks in simple ways.

The teacher–facilitator is familiar with the design, implementation and management of Moodle 2.0 courses, including the settings of conditional activities.

Students have basic digital competences and use of Web 2.0 tools (forums, wikis, social bookmarking and social networks).

2.5.2 Devices

The implementation of the *SSW4LL* format in a distributed learning environment requires an Internet connection and one of the following sets of equipment, according to the students' location:

- a workstation, a webcam and a headphone set if the students are in a fixed location;
- smartphones, portable game consoles or tablets if the students are in a mobile learning environment;
- laptops, smartphones, ultra-mobile PCs or tablets together with the use of sensor network nodes, contact-less smart cards, RFID (Radio Frequency Identification) and QR (Quick Response) codes, if the students are in a ubiquitous learning environment (as an extension of the *SSW4LL* format that would consider the organisation of the learning environment in both real spaces/elements—physical location, participants and paper-based learning material—and virtual spaces/elements—HTML pages, interactive learning materials and Web-based tools).

2.5.3 Recommendations for an Optimal Implementation of the Format

The format *SSW4LL* is very flexible for both the teacher–facilitator and the learners. Anyhow, crucial factors for the success of the experience are (1) thorough organisation and management of the necessary hardware and software; (2) an adequate familiarisation of the students with the learning environment (technology, tools and learning approach); (3) a light e-moderation by the facilitator, in order to provide a modulation of self-regulated and shared learning on the basis of the students' silent and/or expressed requests, with the aim of supporting participants' high motivation.

2.5.4 Workflow and Procedures

The process of feasibility check and of implementation of the format is made up of two phases, as described in the following.

1. *Phase 1*: *Feasibility check (Fc)*
   The check of the feasibility of the planned learning experience is carried out by the teacher–facilitator with the learning technologist and the ICT technician through a double check (Fc1 and Fc2) to verify the correct functioning of all the necessary hardware, software and networks.

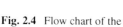

Fig. 2.4 Flow chart of the implementation process of the *SSW4LL* format

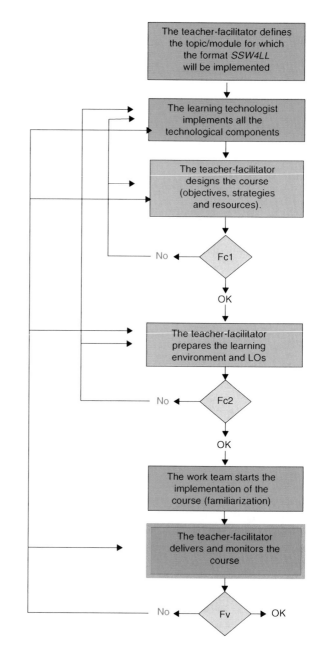

2. *Phase 2: Format validation (Fv)*

The validation of the format as a whole is carried out by the ICT technician on the hardware, software and networks used, on the basis of a checklist, and by the teacher–facilitator, on the basis of evaluation and assessment (Fig. 2.4).

2.5.5   Use Case Scenario

John is a senior university lecturer in the history of music. He is a strongly motivated self-directed learner, as well. Anyhow, work overload does not leave him much time to update his PLE as he would like to. Time constraints and information overload are difficult issues for John, who is considering to look for a flexible course to meet his needs as a lifelong learner. Since he has thought of dedicating some time to deepen his knowledge of jazz for a bit, he decides to enrol in a refresher course on this topic that his university is offering entirely online, in a learner-centred approach, over 2 weeks. He is not new to technology-enhanced learning, but this is the first time he uses some of the tools provided within the course. For this reason, as soon as he receives his logins to Moodle and SMW, and the invitation to join in the Diigo course group and Google+ from the teacher–facilitator, he creates his accounts in these two. He is familiar with social bookmarking and has already used Diigo search before, but he is not a keen user of social networks. He already knows he is not going to use Google+ that much during the course. Anyhow, he decides to enter Moodle to have a look at the video tutorials that the facilitator has suggested for these first two warm-up days of technological familiarisation; he is also curious to meet the other participants and happy to introduce himself in the participants' forum. When he logs in Moodle, he finds a welcoming post by the facilitator and his reminder to complete the entry survey to express expectations and personal background. John carries out the survey and suddenly he visualises a video presentation of the course and a list of tutorials, user's manuals and sandboxes. John is free to choose among them and spends some time in Semantic MediaWiki sandbox; semantic annotation appears decisively useful to his goals in terms of knowledge construction and management, but he needs more time to practice.

At the end of the first two days, John has met 10 course peers in the forum (introductions), in Diigo and in Google+. He has shared a couple of resources in Diigo (using Diigo highlighter, sticky notes and tags) and has created the course circle in his Google+ account. He realises that, through his contacts in these social tools, he is already able to easily get to new resources and users related to the history of jazz.

At the beginning of the third day, the facilitator invites participants to find out more in Moodle: learning modules are ready to be accessed. What is new to John is that learning is personalised: John logs in Moodle and can visualise the quiz *How do you prefer to learn?*; he completes it, he obtains a feedback about his learning style, he confirms it in a "choice" tool for the corresponding most suitable learning sequence and the system starts his sequence of LOs. John is able to visualise the various LOs as he proceeds, and at the end he can move among them as he prefers. This allows John to both take advantage of a personalised scaffolded learning path and to decide autonomously what to do and how much time and effort to spend. He is also aware of his prior knowledge on the topic because he has answered a true/false quiz. He is free to spend as much time as he needs on each learning resource, and he can self-check his knowledge and skills as many times as he feels like through the self-assessment test. Besides, he comments in the forum, he participates in a video hangout in Google+, he collects and annotates considerations in Semantic

MediaWiki and he follows what is going on in the Diigo course group by the Diigo widgets in Moodle. At the end of the first week, John realises he has learnt more about jazz, but, above all, he has had the chance to learn to use new tools that can support him in managing his PLE.

2.6   SWOT Analysis

The following matrix highlights strengths, weaknesses, opportunities and threats of the *SSW4LL* format (Table 2.3).

2.7   Summary

This chapter has started the development of the characterisation of a PLE as a LLL tool by detailing the *SSW4LL* format. After an overview about the aims, possible scenarios and elements of the format, a motivated choice of adult lifelong learners' needs that *SSW4LL* aims to meet has been developed. Subsequently, the learning paradigm and strategies that underpin the *SSW4LL* format have been illustrated. Then, the *SSW4LL* system, the technological architecture, has been presented as a whole made up of components of formal and informal learning environments. The formal learning environment has been devised by Moodle 2.0; a description and an evaluation of Moodle 2.0 features have been provided, with a focus on the potential of its conditional activities as a suitable mechanism of learning adaptation. Concurrently, this part has identified the benefits of the FSLSM, which was selected as the most suitable learning style model for the use in LMSs. The elements of the informal learning environment, Semantic MediaWiki, Diigo and Google+, have been presented, and their implications within the *SSW4LL* format have been discussed. The next section of the chapter has dealt with the organisation of the format: the resources needed, a user case scenario and a flow chart of the steps of the format implementation have been outlined. Finally, a SWOT analysis has provided evaluation elements for the format.

As a whole, this chapter has allowed to achieve the following results. The *SSW4LL* format offers an adaptive, modular, flexible and integrated architecture,

Table 2.3 SWOT analysis of the *SSW4LL* format

Internal	Strengths	Weaknesses
	• Scaffolded self-regulated learning. • Personalised and flexible learning. • Novel tools for the characterisation of adult lifelong learners' PLEs.	• Possible technological issues can cause demotivation.
External	Opportunities	Threats
	• Growing availability of open software and learning materials. • Increasing individuals' awareness of the importance of a LLL vision.	• If the format is applied by a teacher-centred approach, its aims and flexibility are affected. • Insufficient Internet connection.

compatible with future Moodle releases and easy to use for teachers-facilitators. The influence of the informal learning components of the *SSW4LL* system is strong: where social software gives users freedom to choose their own processes and supports the collaboration of adult lifelong learners *anytime, anywhere*, Semantic Web technology gives the possibility to structure information for easy retrieval, reuse and exchange between different systems and tools.

The format is conceived to empower adult lifelong learners by facilitating the acquisition of some of the skills necessary for the twenty-first century.

References

Bratsas, C., Kapsas, G., Konstantinidis, S., Koutsouridis, G., Bamidis, P. (2009). A semantic wiki within Moodle for Greek medical education. In *Proceedings of the 22nd IEEE International Symposium on Computer-Based Medical Systems* (pp. 1–6). Washington, DC: IEEE Computer Society Press.

Bruner, J. (1960). *The Process of Education*. Cambridge, MA: Harvard University Press.

Carver, C. A., Howard, R. A., & Lane, W. D. (1999). Addressing different learning styles through course hypermedia. *IEEE Transactions on Education, 42*, 33–38.

Cooch, M. (2010). *Moodle 2.0 First look*. Birmingham: Packt.

Corneli, J. & Danoff, C.J. (2011). *Paragogy: synergizing individual and organizational learning.* Retrieved 29th September 2011 from http://en.wikiversity.org/wiki/User:Arided/ParagogyPaper.

Cummins, J., Brown, K., & Sayers, D. (2007). *Literacy, technology, and diversity: Teaching for success in changing times*. Boston, MA: Allyn & Bacon/Pearson.

Drexler, W. (2010). The networked student model for construction of personal learning environments: Balancing teacher control and student autonomy. *Australasian Journal of Educational Technology, 26*, 369–385.

El Helou, S., Salzmann, C., & Gillet, D. (2010). The 3A personalized, contextual and relation-based recommender system. *Journal of Universal Computer Science, 16*, 2179–2195.

European Commission. (2011). *Action Plan on Adult Learning: Achievements and results 2008–2010*. Brussels: European Commission.

European Parliament; Council of the European Union. (2006). Recommendation of the European Parliament and of the Council of 18 December 2006 on key competences for lifelong learning. *Official Journal of the European Union*, 10–18.

Felder, R. M., & Silverman, L. K. (1988). Learning and teaching styles in engineering education. *Engineering Education, 78*, 674–681.

Felder, R. M., & Soloman, B. A. (1997). *Index of learning styles questionnaire*. Retrieved August 30, 2011 from http://www.engr.ncsu.edu/learningstyles/ilsweb.html.

Felder, R. M., & Spurlin, J. (2005). Reliability and validity of the index of learning styles: A meta-analysis. *International Journal of Engineering Education, 21*, 103–112.

Fulantelli, G., & Oprea, L. (2011). *SLOOP2desc Preparing teachers for a competence-based education system*. Galati: Europlus Publishing.

Giovannella, C. (2008). *Learning 2.0?* Atti del V congresso Sie-l.

Graf, S. (2007). *Adaptivity in learning management systems focusing on learning styles*. Vienna: Vienna University of Technology.

Graf, S., Kinshuk, & Ives, C. (2010). A flexible mechanism for providing adaptivity based on learning styles in learning management systems. In *Proceeding of the IEEE International Conference on Advanced Learning Technologies* (ICALT) (pp. 30–34). Sousse: IEEE Computer Society.

Herzig, D. M., & Ell, B. (2010). Semantic MediaWiki in Operation: Experiences with building a semantic portal. In *Proceedings of the 9th International Semantic Web Conference* (ISWC-10) (pp. 114–128). Berlin: Springer.

Knowles, M. S. (1970). *The modern practice of adult education: Andragogy versus pedagogy.* New York: Associated Press.

Kolb, D. A. (1984). *Experiential Learning: experience as the source of learning and development.* New Jersey: Prentice-Hall.

Krötzsch, M., Vrandecic, D., Völkel, M., Haller, H. & Studer, R. (2007). Semantic Wikipedia. *Journal of Web Semantics* 5/2007, pp. 251–261.

Kuljis, J., & Liu, F. (2005). A comparison of learning style theories on the suitability for elearning. In M. H. Hamza (Ed.), *Proceedings of the IASTED Conference on Web Technologies, Applications, and Services* (pp. 191–197). Calgary, AB: ACTA Press.

Leadbeater, C. (2004). *Personalisation through participation: A new script for public services.* London: Demos.

Leo, T., Manganello, F., & Chen, N.-S. (2010). From the learning work to the learning adventure. In *Proceedings of EDEN 2010 Annual Conference* (pp 9–11), Valencia, Spain.

Leone, S. (2009). PLE: *A brick in the construction of a lifelong learning society. Technology supported environment for personalised learning methods and case studies.* Hershey, PA: IGI Global.

Leone, S., & Guazzaroni, G. (2010). *Pedagogical sustainability of interoperable formal and informal learning environments. Developing and utilizing e-learning applications.* Hershey, PA: IGI Global.

Leone, S., & Leo, T. (2011). The synergy of paper-based and digital material for ubiquitous foreign language learners. *Knowledge Management & E-Learning: An International Journal (KM&EL), 3,* 319–341.

Limongelli, C., Sciarrone, F., & Vaste, G. (2011). Personalized e-learning in Moodle: The Moodle_LS System. *Journal of e-Learning and Knowledge Society, 7,* 49–58.

Lin, T.-J. (2011). Review of Moodle 2.0. *Language Learning & Technology, 15,* 27–33.

Lubesky, R. (2006). *The present and future of Personal Learning Environments (PLE).* Optusnet.

Maharey, S. (2007). *Organising for personalising learning.* Wellington: Ministry of Education media release, New Zealand Government.

Modritscher, F., Krumay, B., Helou, S. E., Gillet, D., Nussbaumer, A., Albert, D., et al. (2011, July). May I suggest? Three PLE recommender strategies in comparison. *Proceedings of the PLE Conference 2011* (pp. 1–11), Southampton, UK.

Monachesi, P., & Markus, F. T. (2010, May). Socially driven ontology enrichment for eLearning. *Proceedings of the Language Resources and Evaluation Conference,* Valletta, Malta.

Monachesi, P., Markus, F. T., Westerhout, E. N., Osenova, P., & Simov, K. (2011). Supporting formal and informal learning through domain ontologies. *e-Education, e-Business, e-Management, and e-Learning – IEEE, 2*(2), 117–121.

Oppermann, R., & Simm, H. (1994). Adaptability: User-initiated individualization. In R. Oppermann (Ed.), *Adaptive user support: Ergonomic design of manually and automatically adaptable software* (pp. 14–64). Hillsdale, NJ: Lawrence Erlbaum Associates.

Page, L., Brin, S., Motwani, R., & Winograd, T. (1999). *The pagerank citation ranking: Bringing order to the web* (Technical Report 1999–66). Stanford, CA: Stanford InfoLab.

Posea, V., & Trausan-Matu, S. (2010). Bringing the social semantic Web to the personal learning environment. In *Proceedings of the 10th IEEE International Conference on Advanced Learning Technologies (ICALT).* Sousse, Tunisia: IEEE Computer Society.

Varisco, B. M. (2002). *Costruttivismo socio-culturale Genesi filosofiche, sviluppi psico-pedagogici, applicazioni didattiche.* Roma: Carocci.

Vygotsky, L. S. (1986). *Thought and language.* Cambridge, MA: MIT Press.

Westerhout, E. N., Monachesi, P., Markus, F. T., & Posea, V. (2010). Enhancing the learning process: Qualitative validation of an informal learning support system consisting of a knowledge discovery and a social learning component. In M. Wolpers, P. A. Kirschner, M. Scheffel, et al. (Eds.), *Sustaining TEL: From innovation to learning and practice* (Lecture Notes in Computer Science, Vol. 6383, pp. 374–389). Berlin: Springer.

Zimmerman, B. J. (1990). Self-regulated learning and academic achievement: An overview. *Educational Psychologist, 25,* 3–17.

Chapter 3
Case Study: *SSW4LL 2011*

Abstract The case study that follows describes an experience of implementation of the *SSW4LL* format to deliver the course *Social Semantic Web for Lifelong Learners* (*SSW4LL*) *2011* that the author has held for adult lifelong learners who were expert ICT and/or eLearning professionals, but novice in Social Semantic Web. Design and implementation steps and issues of *SSW4LL 2011* are detailed, and outcomes are discussed. The *SSW4LL* format has been evaluated with respect to its efficiency in supporting adult lifelong learners and making the characterisation of their PLEs easier for them.

The course was held in English because it was addressed to the international community, over 4 weeks, from October 3 to October 28, 2011, entirely online, but the environment has been kept open to all the registered learners. Registered participants were 33 in all, but 7 of them never accessed the course and 5 accessed without progressing; thus, active learners were 21.

3.1 Design

The design of the course was based on the ADDIE Instructional Design model and rapid e-learning tools (Piskurich, 2006; Savery & Duffy, 1994). The approach adopted was learner-centred and emphasised motivational factors. Methodology drew entirely on the learning paradigm and strategies of the *SSW4LL* format. Objectives of *SSW4LL 2011* were let learners acquire knowledge about Social Semantic Web (definition, languages, tools and projects for e-learning), and being able to choose, implement and use Social Semantic Web tools in eLearning paths appropriately.

S. Leone, *Characterisation of a Personal Learning Environment as a Lifelong Learning Tool*, SpringerBriefs in Education, DOI 10.1007/978-1-4614-6274-3_3,
© Springer Science+Business Media New York 2013

SSW4LL 2011 was developed over four weekly modules:

1. week 0 (October 3–10)—Technology familiarisation with the learning environment;
2. week 1 (October 10–16)—From the Social Web to the Semantic Web and to the Social Semantic Web: evolution and definitions;
3. week 2 (October 17–23)—The Semantic Web;
4. week 3 (October 24–28)—Where the Social Web meets the Semantic Web.

The course was monitored through the following tests and surveys:

1. an entry survey, at the beginning of week 0, that aimed to explore participants' expectations on the course and their concept of learning and PLE;
2. the survey *How do you characterise your PLE?*, at the beginning of week 1, that aimed to take a snapshot of the characterisation of learners' PLEs at the beginning of the learning path;
3. the entry self-assessment test *How do you prefer to learn?*, at the beginning of week 1, that aimed to determine learners' learning styles[1];
4. the entry self-assessment test *Determine your prior knowledge*, at the beginning of week 1;
5. the *Self-assessment week 1* test, at the end of week 1 to self-check the knowledge and skills acquired during the first module;
6. the feedback surveys *How did you like week 1?*, at beginning of week 2, that aimed to evaluate the ongoing impact of *SSW4LL* implicit and explicit personalisation tools (i.e. adaptive mechanism for the suggestion of the learning path and SSW) on the characterisation of learners' PLEs;
7. the forum *Comments on week 1 work and tools*, at beginning of week 2, where learners were invited to post their comments about week 1 work and tools, to contribute to the improvement of the learning environment;
8. the *Self-assessment week 2* test, at the end of week 2 to self-check the knowledge and skills acquired during the second module;
9. the feedback surveys *How did you like week 2?*, at beginning of week 3, that aimed to evaluate the ongoing impact of *SSW4LL* implicit and explicit personalisation tools on the characterisation of learners' PLEs;
10. the forum *Comments on week 2 work and tools*, at beginning of week 3, where learners were invited to post their comments about week 2 work and tools, to contribute to the improvement of the learning environment;
11. the *Self-assessment week 3* test, at the end of week 3 to self-check the knowledge and skills acquired during the third module;
12. the survey *Final feedback*, to evaluate the effectiveness of the course in terms of participants' satisfaction.

Self-assessment tests allowed unlimited attempts and could be used as summative self-assessment as well. Anyhow, a final cooperative work in SMW was foreseen, too.

---

[1] See Sect. 2.4.1.

3.2 Implementation

3.2.1 Implementation of the SSW4LL System

The implementation of the *SSW4LL* system started with the components of the formal learning environment. Moodle 2.0.4 was installed on the author's space on a remote server (http://www.elearningplace.it/tesisab). This release of Moodle 2.0 was chosen as the most suitable to avoid conflicts with the different versions of PHP and MySQL used by the provider.

The graphical interface of Moodle was personalised by modifying in HTML and PHP the theme that had been selected; colours and fonts were chosen in order to express informality and welcome. Further, a logo was created with the abbreviation of the title of the course and the replacement of "for" with "4", in the Web fashion.

In the home page of Moodle, an *About* page gave an overview of the course and allowed to share the event by social icons. A *Skype in the classroom* icon was embedded as well, as a link to the corresponding Skype projects space in which *SSW4LL 2011* has been included (http://education.skype.com/projects/1168)[2] (Fig. 3.1). Finally, in the same page, a *sign up* link took to a registration form; this form was created by using one of the most reliable free Web-based services; it was personalised, and a Captcha code was installed, too, to avoid spam (Fig. 3.2).

Fig. 3.1 *SSW4LL 2011* homepage in Moodle

---

[2] Skype was included as an efficient way to rapidly and informally communicate.

Fig. 3.2 Registration form to *SSW4LL 2011*

Subsequently, the components of the informal learning environment were implemented. Semantic MediaWiki required the installation of MediaWiki, first. Their latest releases (1.17.0 for MediaWiki and 1.6.0 for Semantic MediaWiki) and the extension WYSIWYG as a user-friendly editor for Semantic MediaWiki were installed.

A Diigo *SSW4LL* group was created and two Diigo widgets were implemented in the home page of the course: a *Diigo SSW4LL group's best content*, the group's linkroll that displayed the latest (linked) resources that the participants had bookmarked in Diigo *SSW4LL* group; a *Diigo SSW4LL group's tags* that showed all the tags that *SSW4LL*'s participants had used in the group (Fig. 3.3). Learners had to sign in Diigo before joining in the Diigo *SSW4LL* group, which was set as a close group and required an invitation to access.

Before the beginning of the course, Google+ had just completed the testing of its beta release, thus users were free to sign in.

SSW4LL 2011 formal and informal learning environments were integrated by embedding Diigo widgets and links to Semantic MediaWiki and Google+ in Moodle. The implementation of a Single Sign On (SSO) was considered, but the author did not have a CAS server; moreover, preceding direct experiences of implementation of eLearning environments had posed the following issues:

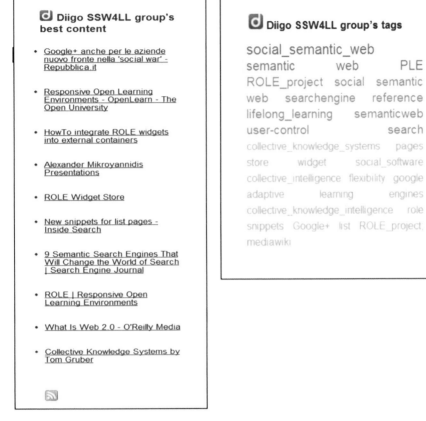

Fig. 3.3 Diigo widgets in *SSW4LL 2011* homepage, in Moodle

- the SSO very often creates technical problems to the learners, who are not particularly familiar with troubleshooting;
- typically, a high number of learners lose their Moodle password and have to follow the default procedure to recover it;
- when a SSO is implemented, all Moodle users are registered on an authentication platform as well (e.g. CAS server). When they log in Moodle, their access is filtered through this authentication platform; if the data present in Moodle and in the authentication platform are not synchronised, users' login is denied;
- consequent negative effects are users' frustration (most of the times they attribute this inconvenience to their poor digital skills), that is particularly damaging in an eLearning environment, and a waste of time and energy for troubleshooting.

In the end, social semantic software could be smoothly integrated in the architecture by using widgets and links; additionally, learners could autonomously opt for allowing their login sessions to Semantic MediaWiki, Diigo and Google+ to never expire.

3.2.2 Implementation of the Course SSW4LL 2011

The course was promoted virally by the following several means:

1. the indexing of the home page of Moodle, where an extensive overview of the *SSW4LL 2011* objectives, scheduled modules, learning environment and staff's bios was provided;
2. many social icons embedded in the home page of Moodle, among which the icon of Google+, that allowed site visitors to share the event in their networks;
3. a facilitator's video presentation of the course that was posted in the author's Youtube channel and viralised;
4. submission to the *Skype in the classroom* platform;
5. the link to the *Skype in the classroom* platform, in the home page of Moodle;
6. a public post in Google+ that was shared by other users in Facebook and Twitter;
7. a post in the *Sloop2desc* and *Qualified online tutors* Facebook groups;
8. emails to colleagues of various universities;
9. submission to the Moodle Hub, where projects that are developed by Moodle are presented.

Concurrently, the formal learning environment was set up. The following sections were created:

1. *News and announcements*, a forum with posts from the facilitator only.
2. *Section 1—Introduction and guidelines* (Fig. 3.4) that contained the entry survey (to explore participants' expectations on the course and their concept of learning and PLE), a facilitator's video presentation of the course (Fig. 3.5[3]), a list of links to guidelines, tutorials (in different formats) and sandboxes of the tools of the *SSW4LL* system that participants were going to use and definitions of LLL, life-long learners and PLE that aimed to provide an initial common understanding on these concepts. This section was available as of week 0 (October 3), in which the technology familiarisation took place. However, when learners entered the course in week 0, they could visualise only the entry survey; once they had completed it, the adaptive mechanism showed them all the other parts of the section. The aim was to collect participants' uninfluenced expectations on the course and their view of the concept of PLE.
3. *Section 2—Useful links*, related to the topic of the course (e.g. W3C, FOAF, SIOC, etc.). Learners could visualise this section as of week 1 (October 10), when the course on Social Semantic Web started.
4. *Section 3—Learning modules* (Fig. 3.6) that was introduced by the survey *How do you characterise your PLE?* (for which a date availability restriction—

---

[3]In the figure, the Microsoft Tag is used as the latest evolution of the QR code. It can be decodified by a free Microsoft Tag reader (basic version), downloadable at http://tag.microsoft.com/what-is-tag/scanning-tags.aspx. The video presentation is also available at http://www.youtube.com/watch?v=9LyyGGOQ9kg.

Home ► My courses ► SSW4LL 2011

Weekly outline

- News and announcements
- Choose the date of our next videohuddle in G+ (week 2)
- Book for our next videohuddle in G+ (week 3). Friday 28th h9.30pm!

Section 1 - Introduction and guidelines

- Entry survey

Restricted (completely hidden, no message): 'Not available until the activity Entry survey is marked complete.'

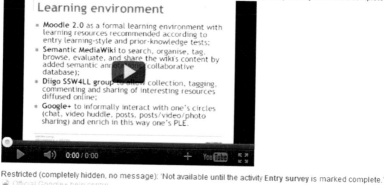

Restricted (completely hidden, no message): 'Not available until the activity Entry survey is marked complete.'
- Official Google+ help centre
Restricted (completely hidden, no message): 'Not available until the activity Entry survey is marked complete.'
- Google+ user-generated manual
Restricted (completely hidden, no message): 'Not available until the activity Entry survey is marked complete.'
- Diigo user's guide
Restricted (completely hidden, no message): 'Not available until the activity Entry survey is marked complete.'
- Semantic MediaWiki's user manual
Restricted (completely hidden, no message): 'Not available until the activity Entry survey is marked complete.'
- Semantic MediaWiki sandbox
Restricted (completely hidden, no message): 'Not available until the activity Entry survey is marked complete.'
- EU Lifelong Learning Programme 2007-2013 - Glossary
Restricted (completely hidden, no message): 'Not available until the activity Entry survey is marked complete.'
- EU Glossary of eLearning
Restricted (completely hidden, no message): 'Not available until the activity Entry survey is marked complete.'

Fig. 3.4 *SSW4LL 2011* Section 1

October 10—had been set in the back end) and by the self-assessment tests *How do you prefer to learn?* and *Determine your prior knowledge* that learners could visualise on completion of the survey. Subsequently, the section was subdivided into 3 weeks in which the respective abovementioned learning modules were developed. Different learning sequences were made available; they were tailored on the basis of the 16 learning profiles resulting from the combination of the

Fig. 3.5 The video presentation of *SSW4LL 2011*

Section 3 - Learning modules

How do you characterise your PLE?
Restricted (completely hidden, no message): 'Available from 10 ottobre 2011.'
How do you prefer to learn?
Restricted: 'Not available until the activity How do you characterise your PLE? is marked complete. Available from 10 ottobre 2011.'
Determine your prior knowledge
Restricted: 'Not available until the activity How do you characterise your PLE? is marked complete. Available from 10 ottobre 2011.'

Week 1: 10th -16th October

From the Social Web to the Semantic Web and to the Social Semantic Web: evolution and definitions

Commentary
Restricted (completely hidden, no message): 'Not available until the activity How do you prefer to learn? is marked complete.'
Choose your learning sequence
Restricted (completely hidden, no message): 'Not available until the activity Commentary is marked complete.'

Information R/evolution

Restricted (completely hidden, no message): 'Not available until you achieve a required score in Choose your learning sequence.'

Do you agree with this image of the information revolution?
Restricted (completely hidden, no message): 'Not available until the activity Choose your learning sequence is marked complete.'
Where the Social Web meets the Semantic Web
Restricted (completely hidden, no message): 'Not available until the activity Do you agree with this image of the information revolution? is marked complete.'
The Social Web
Restricted (completely hidden, no message): 'Not available until the activity Where the Social Web meets the Semantic Web. is marked complete.'
The Semantic Web
Restricted (completely hidden, no message): 'Not available until the activity The Social Web is marked complete.'
The Social Semantic Web
Restricted (completely hidden, no message): 'Not available until the activity The Semantic Web is marked complete.'
Self-assessment week 1
Restricted (completely hidden, no message): 'Not available until the activity The Social Semantic Web is marked complete.'
Reflection quiz
Restricted (completely hidden, no message): 'Not available until the activity Self-assessment week 1 is marked complete.'
Learning sequence 2
Restricted (completely hidden, no message): 'Not available until you achieve a required score in Choose your learning sequence.'
Learning sequence 3
Restricted (completely hidden, no message): 'Not available until you achieve a required score in Choose your learning sequence.'

Fig. 3.6 *SSW4LL 2011* Section 3

eight style categories of the FSLSM (Felder and Silverman, 1988).[4] Further, within each learning sequence LOs were adaptively showed to learners progressively, on the basis of their self-paced learning time.

5. *Section 4—Collaborative and cooperative work*, through:

   - *discussions*, a forum where learners could discuss topics with their peers and facilitator, and propose new applications and relevant scenarios;
   - *technical help*, a forum where learners could ask their peers and technical eTutor for any kind of help inherent the course and support each other;
   - *additional resources*, suggestions of interesting and useful learning material collected collaboratively by Diigo;
   - *networking*, informal learning by Google+;
   - *cooperative work*, co-writing of a collective final work, initially proposed and agreed by the participants, in Semantic MediaWiki.

On the compilation of the registration form, participants were sent an email of confirmation individually, with logins to Moodle and Semantic MediaWiki, invitations to join in Diigo *SSW4LL* group and Google+ and welcoming hints to warm-up in *SSW4LL 2011*.

Through the whole course, facilitator's light e-moderation and technical eTutor's punctual support scaffolded self-paced participants' activities. At the end of each week, video hangouts were held in Google+ to favour informal brainstorming sessions, and enhance warm-up and active participation. During the last video hangout, Dr. Alexander Mikroyannidis of the KMi, Open University (UK), was invited to present the main outcomes of the ROLE project,[5] in which he is involved as a researcher.

3.3 Evaluation and Discussion

At the beginning of week 0, the entry survey explored participants' expectations on *SSW4LL 2011* and their concept of learning and PLE. Twenty-one of the registered learners carried out the survey. Their resulting average profile showed that the course format might have met their needs. As a matter of fact, 11 (52.4%) participants were ICT experts and 6 (28.6%) eLearning professionals; 10 (47.6%) had 6–10 years of professional experience, 6 (28.6%) 11–20 years and 5 (23.8%) more than 20 years; 11 (52.4%) were between 36 and 45 years old, and the remaining 10 (47.6%) were between 46 and 55 years old; 16 (76.2%) affirmed that their PLE is made up of digital resources, non-digital resources, family and social relations and that learning is an adventure, rather than a path (5, 23.8%). Thirteen

---

[4] See Sect. 2.4.1.
[5] See Sect. 1.3.5.

(61.9%) were novice learners of SSW, while the others had either self-learnt (6, 28.6%) or followed other courses on this subject (2, 9.5%); they decided to join *SSW4LL 2011* out of curiosity (14, 66.6%), personal culture (13, 61.9%) and for professional enhancement (14, 66.6%). From the course they expected above all effective contents (11, 52.4%), situated learning and collaborative/cooperative work (10, 47.6%), handy and real acquisition of competences in the field (9, 42.9%) and interaction and personalised learning (7, 33.3%). Surprisingly enough considering the respondents' profile, only one-third of them expected to have a personalised learning environment. At this first step, this could indicate that either they had never experienced a personalised course before or that they were distrustful about what *SSW4LL 2011* promised to provide.

At the beginning of week 1 the survey *How do you characterise your PLE?* opened the learning path. Respondents decreased to 17, but 15 of them (88.2%) affirmed that, as lifelong learners, they had never followed a course that offered adaptive learning. This explained their limited expectations in terms of personalised learning in *SSW4LL 2011* expressed in the entry survey, in the preceding week. The other two participants had followed courses with adaptive learning, and one of them declared that experience had made her more responsible about her personal learning, and that learning was more effective. The survey also emphasised that participants usually characterise their PLE mostly by the Office suite (13, 76.5%), social networks (11, 64.7%), blogs and forums (10, 58.8%), followed by RSS feeds, ebooks and books (8, 47%), wikis, social bookmarking, newspapers and colleagues (7, 41.2%), friends (5, 29.4%), podcasts and TV/radio (4, 23.5%), aggregators and family (3, 17.6%) and vlogs (1, 5.9%). Finally, learners manage digital information overload in their PLEs mainly by links (11, 64.7%) and social network tools (e.g. follow, I like, tags) (10, 58.8%); some use repositories (8, 47%), a few use aggregators (5, 29.4%), very few use backlinks, permalinks and semantic annotation tools (2, 11.8%) and none use metadata. These last results highlighted learners' unfamiliarity with semantic tools, and a preference for informal and user-friendly tools as those present in Google+ are.

Once that participants had completed the survey *How do you characterise your PLE?*, the self-assessment test *How do you prefer to learn?* appeared as a result of the adaptive mechanism that had been activated in the back end by the conditional activities. Respondents decreased again. 15 learners answered the test.[6] The participants resulted in being made up of 14 (93.3%) strongly reflective, 13 (86.7%) strongly global and 11 (73.3%) quite intuitive learners; 8 (53.3%) moderately verbal learners, 7 (46.7%) moderately sensing and visual learners, 2 (13.4%) weakly sequential learners and 1 (6.7%) weakly active learner. The combination of the learners' choices in the test generated the following learning profiles:

1. Reflective + intuitive + visual + global (5 learners, 33.3%)
2. Reflective + sensing + verbal + global (4 learners, 26.7%)

---

[6]This self-assessment test was set as described in Sect. 2.4.1.

3. Reflective + intuitive + verbal + sequential (2 learners, 13.4%)
4. Reflective + sensing + visual + global (2 learners, 13.4%)
5. Reflective + intuitive + verbal + global (1 learner, 6.7%)
6. Active + intuitive + verbal + global (1 learner, 6.7%)

This test enabled the different learning sequences that had been designed. From this point on participants progressed at their own pace, scaffolded by the adaptive mechanism of conditional activities, by weekly self-assessment tests that could be repeated an unlimited number of times, by a few posts that the facilitator used also to promote active participation in the *Collaborative and cooperative work* section and by the weekly video hangouts. At the end of week 1, most of the learners had int.oduced themselves in the forum, but interaction was poor. Some apologised and explained that they were extremely motivated and interested in the course, but that their difficulties in the English language blocked their spontaneity. Most of the learners were Italian, but a British and a Malaysian took part to the course, too. During the design of the learning environment, this issue had been foreseen and a link to Google Translator had been included in *Section 2—Useful links* in Moodle. Nevertheless, participants' interaction in the forum and in Semantic MediaWiki was inhibited through the whole course, while Moodle logs showed their active accesses to the learning materials.

At beginning of week 2, the feedback survey *How did you like week 1?* and the forum *Comments on week 1 work and tools* let evaluate the ongoing impact of *SSW4LL* implicit and explicit personalisation tools on the characterisation of learners' PLEs. The same kind of survey and forum were used at the beginning of week 3 (*How did you like week 2?* and *Comments on week 2 work and tools*). Observing and comparing the results of the two feedback surveys (Table 3.1), a first consideration is that the survey on week 1 was completed by only 7 learners, while in the second survey they were 12. A reason for this could be that some of the learners simply skipped the first survey and jumped directly to week 3 learning sequence. This could be possible because the initial *Commentary* of weekly modules showed automatically on the first day of the corresponding week. Thus, some learners could have preferred to complete their learning sequence of week 3 before going back to week 2 and complete the initial feedback survey. In any case, a positive deduction is that the *SSW4LL* format provided a guided and personalised delivery of the course, but it also allowed learners to move freely according to their interests and needs once the limited time of *restricted availability on a date* feature had expired. Second, a comparison of the learners' percentage feedbacks for the two weeks shows an evident improvement of their awareness and achievements, even though the issues suggested by answers 2 require to be clarified. The comments that respondents posted in the above-mentioned forums highlight that a common issue for all the respondents in both weeks was personal time constraints, immediately followed by an insufficient mastery of the English language that made learners insecure in expressing themselves publicly and spontaneously. On the other hand, they affirmed: "the course is very interesting and full of resources", "the tools are very interesting", "I found the first week of the course very interesting, because it allowed me to

Table 3.1 Results of the feedback surveys *How did you like week 1?* and *How did you like week 2?*

| | | Week 1 | | Week 2 | |
| | | Results | | Results | |
n	Answers	(7)	%	(12)	%
1	The suggestion of the learning sequence and the SSW tools were completely useless to characterise my PLE, because I can do it myself.	2	28.6	1	8.3
2	The suggestion of the learning sequence and the SWW tools did not contribute that much in characterising my PLE, partly because I already know how I learn better and I already use an aggregator to filter and network my knowledge, and partly because I did not participate actively in the course.	1	14.3	4	33.3
3	The suggestion of the learning sequence and the SSW tools were quite helpful to characterise my PLE: the adaptive learning sequence made me more aware of the way I learn, and the SWW tools gave me an overview of the means to filter and network the knowledge I am interested in. Unfortunately, I have not had the time to use SSW tools yet.	1	14.3	2	16.7
4	I have used the suggested learning sequence and the SWW tools, and I have found them useful to characterise my PLE. The adaptive learning sequence made me completely aware of the way I learn, and the SWW tools introduced me to a new way to filter the knowledge I am interested in and share it in my networks. I would like to practise more, though.	2	28.6	4	33.3
5	The suggestion of the learning sequence and the SSW tools absolutely enhanced the characterisation of my PLE, because they guided me and supported me in filtering and networking the knowledge I am interested in.	1	14.3	1	8.3

learn a whole new world for me, which is online learning", "the real problem for me is the learning time that mixes with work time. I'd like to learn how to optimize this aspect. I'm happy to have found my learning way through the activities of the week 1. I believe that this will help me in finding the suitable teaching tools for me", "thanks for the opportunity and the interesting topics presented. I also have very little time in this period, but I hope that the course still remains online for quite a while to give me the opportunity to complete it", "also for me, time is a problem but, if the material will remain available for a few weeks I can review everything. I have already put in my PLE Diigo, and I would also start using Semantic MediaWiki", "I joined this course too late, and my English is not so fluent to feel me comfortable in active forum participation. Anyway I thanks you all for your great job", "this course was very *interessante* .... I have not yet grasped all the latest news, but I have started to redefine my PLE using the new tools discovered in this activity".

At the end of *SSW4LL 2011*, the survey *Final feedback* aimed to evaluate the effectiveness of the course in terms of participants' satisfaction and sense of achievement, and thus to validate the *SSW4LL* format. The survey aimed to highlight the overall impact of *SSW4LL* on this cluster of adult lifelong learners, the difficulties arisen, the advantages of adopting an adaptive mechanism and Social Semantic Web tools to characterise learners' PLEs and the outcomes in terms of LLL. The survey consisted of nine multiple choice questions and two open-ended comments at the end (a 5-point Likert scale—strongly agree, agree, neutral, disagree and strongly disagree—was used). Eight learners completed the final feedback survey. The overall learners' perception was extremely positive. Even though some affirmed that the course was tiring (3, 37.5%) and difficult (4, 50%), they considered this learning experience as interesting (8, 100%), new (7, 87.5%), useful (7, 87.5%) and amusing (7, 87.5%). The features that they appreciated most were personalised learning (8, 100%) and flexible and effective contents (7, 87.5%); they also found that the course offered handy and real acquisition of competences in the field and interaction (6, 75%). Collaborative and cooperative work and situated learning were indicated with less emphasis (5, 62.5%).

In relation to their satisfaction with *SSW4LL 2011* tools as means to characterise their PLEs, 4 (50%) participants stated that they had used the suggested learning sequence and the Social Semantic Web tools, and they had found them useful. The adaptive learning sequence had made them completely aware of the way they learn, and the Social Semantic Web tools introduced them to a new way to filter the knowledge they are interested in and to share it in their networks. They would like to practise more, though.

In detail, *SSW4LL 2011* tools learners used most for informal learning were Diigo *SSW4LL* group widgets with the latest bookmarked resources (8, 100%) and the corresponding tags (7, 97.5%) in the homepage of the course; Diigo at its full (6, 75%); Google+ to create their profile (6, 75%), to create circles (5, 62.5%) and to participate in video hangouts (5, 62.5%). Learners were shy, instead, in using Google+ to search and create folders for their interests and to organise video hangouts (3, 37.5%).

Quite neglected was the use of Diigo to search and follow persons with their same interest (2, 25%), Google+ to share others' posts (2, 25%), Google+ to "1+" interesting resources (1, 12.5%), Semantic MediaWiki to co-write and to semantically annotate co-writing (2, 25%).

In the learners' perception, Google+ allowed them to increase the number of their interesting, useful and trusted relations more than Diigo. In Google+ 4 (50%) of them established from 6 to 10 new relations and 1 (12.5%) more than 10 new relations; in Diigo 5 (62.5%) of them established from 0 to 5 new relations and 3 (37.5%) between 6 and 10 new relations.

Difficulties with the English language and personal time constraints (6, 75%) confirmed to be the main issues participants experienced during the course.

At the end of this path 7 (87.5%) participants declared to be gratified because they learnt to do new things, 5 (62.5%) declared to be gratified because they learnt new things and 2 (25%) declared to be frustrated because they could not exploit it at the best. None declared to be deceived because the course did not meet her/his learning needs and expectations.

Respondents' suggestions to improve the course were focussed on a possible version in Italian and on an extension of the scheduled time. Some indicated more explanations about the use of Semantic MediaWiki that could be interpreted as a difficulty in accessing the many guidelines, tutorials and the sandbox that *SSW4LL 2011* provided because they were in English.

Finally, all of the learners would repeat this learning experience to have more time to learn, to deepen, to collaborate with other people, because "it was a very interesting and innovative course", "it was useful and I enjoyed it".

The results obtained from *SSW4LL 2011* come to support the effectiveness of the format implemented. In particular, even though the format was targeted to a cluster of novice learners in the course domain, but professionals in a specific field, research conduced within this research proposed concepts and approaches which are suitable for adult lifelong learners in general, rather than for one specific target within. In this sense, the results of the surveys and tests that were carried out along this experience confirmed that, beyond professional determinants, lifelong learners are self-regulated learners that appreciate the assistance of an adaptive mechanism, especially when topics are complex and unfamiliar.

This experience pointed out that an adaptive system, provided that it is applied in the light of a learner-centred framework, can aid adult lifelong learners to be effectively self-directed and self-regulated, both at domain knowledge level and meta-knowledge level. By fully exploiting Moodle 2.0 adaptation features that in the *SSW4LL* system are based on the detection of learners' learning styles, this LMS can deploy a personalised scaffolded learning environment for self-regulated learners. Further, social software can be smoothly integrated in the architecture by widgets and by allowing login sessions to never expire.

The participants in *SSW4LL 2011* acknowledged the potential of Social Semantic Web tools in characterising their PLEs, but they showed to be ready to use only user-friendly ones. Time constraints is a crucial issue with these learners, and it has to be taken more into account to improve the format.

In technological systems for education a change of direction of technology is evident: technology is not only a means of social exchange, but it turns into the joint design of learning and organisational strategies, and into the growth of learning communities. This approach arises the strong social, pedagogical and technological relation between LLL, e-learning and knowledge management.

3.4   Summary

As a whole, this chapter has allowed to achieve the following results. The *SSW4LL* format has provided a guided and personalised delivery of the course, but it has also allowed learners to move freely according to their interests and needs once the limited time of *restricted availability on a date* feature had expired for the various activities/ modules. Secondly, a comparison of the learners' percentage feedbacks along the course has shown an evident improvement of their awareness and achievements

The outcomes of *SSW4LL 2011* have validated the format implemented. This experience has confirmed that, beyond professional determinants, lifelong learners are self-regulated learners that appreciate the assistance of an adaptive mechanism within a learner-centred framework (especially when topics are complex and unfamiliar) and of user-friendly SSW tools in characterising their PLEs. By fully exploiting Moodle 2.0 adaptation features, this LMS can deploy a personalised scaffolded learning environment for self-regulated learners. Further, social software can be smoothly integrated in the architecture by widgets and by allowing login sessions to never expire.

References

Felder, R. M., & Silverman, L. K. (1988). Learning and teaching styles in engineering education. *Engineering Education, 78*, 674–681.

Piskurich, G. M. (2006). *Rapid instructional design: Learning ID fast and right* (2nd ed.). San Francisco, CA: Pfeiffer.

Savery, J. R., & Duffy, T. M. (1994). Problem based learning: An instructional model and its constructivist framework. *Educational Technology, 8*, 31–8.

Chapter 4
Concluding Remarks

4.1 Conclusions

The diffusing LLL vision and technology revolution have posed increasing attention on personalised learning paths. Dynamic PLEs, instead of organisation-centred LMSs, have been considered as an effective framework for lifelong learners and as nodes of networks of virtual identities that are built by social software. E-learning 2.0 has mediated the shift from formal to informal e-learning, and PLEs have developed relationships between pieces of information in formal as well as informal settings.

This change of perspective manifests in a learning Web where information is distributed across sites, knowledge management becomes an issue, and personalisation requires the support of adaptation and of semantics applied to social components (i.e. the Social Semantic Web).

This research has focussed on the characterisation of adult lifelong learners' PLEs by implicit and explicit tools of personalisation. The synergy of formal and informal learning in the dynamic construction of a lifelong learner's PLE has been explored. The *SSW4LL* (*Social Semantic Web for Lifelong Learners*) format has been devised, and the *SSW4LL* system, built on Moodle 2.0 integrated with an adaptive mechanism (conditional activities) and some tools of Social Semantic Web (Semantic MediaWiki, Diigo and Google+), has been designed, implemented and successfully validated as a device suitable to provide a dynamically personalised learning environment to the lifelong learner.

Results of a comprehensive literature review and the outcomes obtained from *SSW4LL 2011* come to support the effectiveness of the format implemented, and confirm that lifelong learners are self-regulated learners that appreciate the assistance of an adaptive mechanism, especially when topics are complex and unfamiliar, and the potential of user-friendly Social Semantic Web tools in characterising their PLEs. This experience pointed out that, by fully exploiting Moodle 2.0 adaptation features in the light of a learner-centred framework, this LMS can deploy a

S. Leone, *Characterisation of a Personal Learning Environment as a Lifelong Learning Tool*, SpringerBriefs in Education, DOI 10.1007/978-1-4614-6274-3_4,
© Springer Science+Business Media New York 2013

personalised scaffolded learning environment and can aid adult lifelong learners to be effectively self-directed and self-regulated. Further, this research has shown that social software can be smoothly integrated in the architecture by widgets and by allowing login sessions to never expire, and that the integration of social software into formal learning environments can make a qualitative difference to giving adult lifelong learners a sense of ownership and control over their own learning and career planning.

In technological systems for education, a change of direction of technology is evident: technology is not only a means of social exchange, but it turns into the joint design of learning and organisational strategies, and into the growth of learning communities. This approach arises the strong social, pedagogical and technological relation between LLL, e-learning and knowledge management.

This research could open ways for advanced learning systems, which are able to meet the learners' needs and characteristics, merge assets of formal and informal learning environments and provide learners with dynamic personalisation of their PLEs.

4.2 Future Directions

In the future, improvements of the *SSW4LL* system include enabling the integration of additional social semantic tools to tackle differently knowledge management, syndicating resources and trustworthiness, that are actual research issues related to the enhancement of dynamic PLEs. Moreover, in-depth observation could be conducted on how the learning outcomes improve by transferring responsibility for the choice and configuration of the learning environment from the teacher to the learner by social semantic tools.

Appendix: Glossary

Adaptation A process of selection, generation or modification that produces one or more perceivable units in response to a requested uniform resource identifier (URI) in a given delivery context (W3C, 2005).

Adaptive system A system that adapts to the users, automatically based on the system's assumptions about the users' needs (Oppermann, 1994).

Adaptivity In adaptive learning systems, adaptivity consists in increased user's efficiency, effectiveness and satisfaction by greater correspondence between learner, goal and characteristics of the system (Graf, Lan, Liu, & Kinshuk, 2009).

Adult education All forms of non-vocational adult learning, whether of a formal, non-formal or informal nature. Formal learning usually takes place in schools, universities or training institutions and leads to a diploma or certificate. Non-formal learning includes free adult education within study circles, projects or discussion groups advancing at their own place, with no examination at the end. Informal learning can be found everywhere (e.g., in families, in the workplace, in theatre groups, at home, etc.) (UNESCO, 1999).

Adult learner A learner participating in adult education (UNESCO, 1999).

AEH (Adaptive Educational Hypermedia): A system that "adapts" the learning path to the learner's profile (Brusilovsky, 1998).

AH (Adaptive Hypermedia): A system that tailors the selection of links or contents to be visualised on the user's goals, abilities, interests, knowledge, context, device used to access the information (Brusilovsky, 1996).

Architecture The software architecture of a program or computing system is the structure or structures of the system. This structure includes software components, the externally visible properties of those components, the relationships among them and the constraints on their use (W3C, 2004d).

Authentication The process of verifying that a potential partner in a conversation is capable of representing a person or organisation (W3C, 2004d).

Backlink A link in one direction implied from the existence of an explicit link in the other direction (W3C, 1995).

S. Leone, *Characterisation of a Personal Learning Environment as a Lifelong Learning Tool*, SpringerBriefs in Education, DOI 10.1007/978-1-4614-6274-3, © Springer Science+Business Media New York 2013

CAS (Central Authentication Service): Single Sign-On protocol (SSO) for the Web that permits a user to access multiple applications while providing his/her credentials (userid and password) only once. It also allows Web applications to authenticate users without gaining access to a user's security credentials, such as a password. The name CAS also refers to a software package that implements this protocol (Jasig, 2011).

Component A software object, meant to interact with other components, encapsulating a certain functionality or a set of functionalities. A component has a clearly defined interface and conforms to a prescribed behaviour common to all components within an architecture (W3C, 2004d).

Configuration A collection of properties which may be changed. A property may influence the behaviour of an entity (W3C, 2004d).

Ecosystem Related to ecology, it is "a biological community of interacting organisms and their physical environment" (http://www.wordreference.com/defini tion/ecosystem). Herein the expression "ecosystem of data" is intended as a specific system of interacting elements and their physical environment, and the expression "ecosystem of participation" is intended as a specific cultural system/ community of interacting users and their sharing environment" (Gruber, 2008). Both terms are an extension of the original definition of ecosystem.

eLearning The use of new multimedia technologies and the Internet to improve the quality of learning by facilitating access to resources and services as well as remote exchanges and collaboration (European Commission's Directorate-General for Education and Culture, 2011).

FOAF (Friend of a Friend): An open, decentralised technology for connecting social Web sites and the people they describe. Specifically, foaf:knows relations can form ties in social networks on the Semantic Web by directly linking two foaf:person (FOAF Project, 2011).

Folksonomy A system of classification derived from the practice and method of collaboratively creating and managing tags to annotate and categorise content (Breslin, Passant, & Decker, 2009).

Heuristics Experience-based techniques for problem solving, learning and discovery. Heuristic methods are used to speed up the process of finding a satisfactory solution, where an exhaustive search is impractical (e.g., a rule of thumb, an educated guess, an intuitive judgment, common sense). In computer science, a heuristic is a technique designed to solve a problem that ignores whether the solution can be proven to be correct, but which usually produces a good solution or solves a simpler problem that contains or intersects with the solution of the more complex problem (Newell & Simon, 1976).

Heuristic classification A widespread method of computation for problem solving, that is made up of three main phases (1) data abstraction from a concrete, particular problem description to a problem class; (2) heuristic mapping onto a hierarchy of pre-enumerated solutions; (3) refinement within this hierarchy. In short, concepts are related in different classification hierarchies by non-hierarchical, uncertain inferences.

"The heuristic classification model characterizes a form of knowledge and reasoning-patterns of familiar problem situations and solutions, heuristically related. In capturing problem situations that tend to occur and solutions that tend to work, this knowledge is essentially experiential, with an overall form that is problem-area independent" (Clancey, 1985, p.10).

HTML (Hypertext markup language): A computer language for representing the contents of a page of hypertext; the language that most Web pages are currently written in (W3C, 1995).

HTTP A computer protocol for transferring information across the Net in such a way as to meet the demands of a global hypertext system. Part of the original design of the Web, continued in a W3C activity, and now a HTTP 1.1 IETF draft standard (W3C, 1999).

Hypermedia HyperMedia and HyperText tend to be used loosely in place of each other. Media other than text typically include graphics, sound and video (W3C, 1995).

Hypertext Non-sequential writing; Ted Nelson's term for a medium that includes links. Nowadays, it includes other media apart from text and is sometimes called hypermedia (W3C, 1999).

Implementation A realisation of a technology in accordance to the principles defined in the technical specifications for this technology. This implementation can be a document, product, application, process, service, system or other entity (W3C, 2005).

Lifelong learners Self-regulated learners, characterised as demonstrating perseverance, initiative and adaptive abilities. Self-regulation relates to an ability to recognise a need for further learning as well as to be proactive in gaining access to and accomplishing learning (Leone, 2010).

Lifelong learning All general education, vocational education and training, non-formal education and informal learning undertaken throughout life, resulting in an improvement in knowledge, skills and competences within a personal, civic, social and/or employment-related perspective. It includes the provision of counselling and guidance services (European Commission, 2002, 2008).

Link A relationship between two resources when one resource (representation) refers to the other resource by means of a URI (W3C, 2004a).

LMS (Learning Management System): Organisation-centred learning spaces where on-line interaction takes place, with any purpose, including learning, between students and teachers (European Commission's Directorate-General for Education and Culture, 2011).

LO (Learning Object): Any digital and non-digital resource that can be reused to support technology-enhanced learning (IEEE, 2000).

Machine understandable/readable Data that is described with tags that associate a meaning to the data (i.e. an "author" tag would describe the author of the document), allowing data to be searched or combined and not just displayed (W3C, 2004e).

Markup language Used to represent documents with a nested, treelike structure. Examples are HTML [HTML4], SVG [SVG] or MathML [MATHML] (W3C, 2000).

Metadata Data about data on the Web, including but not limited to authorship, classification, endorsement, policy, distribution terms, IPR and so on. A significant use for the Semantic Web (W3C, 1999).

MOAT (Meaning Of A Tag): A Semantic Web framework to publish semantically enriched content from free-tagging one, providing a way for users to define meaning(s) of their tag(s) using URIs of Semantic Web resources. Thanks to those relationships between tags and URIs of existing concepts, they can annotate content with those URIs rather than free-text tags, leveraging content into Semantic Web, by linking data together. Moreover, these tag meanings can be shared between people, providing an architecture of participation to define and exchange meanings of tags (as URIs) within a community of users (MOAT-project.org, 2011).

Navigation The process of moving from one node to another through the hypertext web. This is normally done by following links. Various features of a particular browser may make this easier. These include keeping a history of where the user has been, and drawing diagrams of links between nearby nodes (W3C, 1995).

Node A unit of information. Also known as a frame (KMS), card (Hypercard, Notecards). Used with this special meaning in hypertext circles: do not confuse with "node" meaning "network host" (W3C, 1995).

ODF An XML-based file format for representing electronic documents such as spreadsheets, charts, presentations and word processing documents (OASIS, 2011).

Ontology Collection of information, generally including information about classes and properties (W3C, 2004b).

Open source Software whose source code is freely distributed and modifiable by anyone (W3C, 1999).

OWL (Web Ontology Language): A language that can be used to describe the classes and relations between them that are inherent in Web documents and applications (W3C, 2004b).

Permalink (Blend of *permanent link*) is a URL that points to a specific blog or forum entry after it has passed from the front page to the archives. Because a permalink remains unchanged indefinitely, it is less susceptible to link rot. Most modern weblogging and content-syndication software systems support such links (Coates, 2003).

PHP A widely used general-purpose scripting language that is especially suited for Web development and can be embedded into HTML (The PHP Group, 2011).

PLE (Personal Learning Environment): An open system, interconnected with other PLEs and with other external services; it is an activity based learning environment, user-managed and learner-centred. A PLE is a concept rather than specific software, a group of techniques and a variety of tools to gather information, explore and develop relationships between pieces of information. A PLE helps to view the subject as a landscape as well as individual pieces of information, and facilitates the access to and the aggregation, the configuration and the management of the individual's learning experiences (Leone, 2009).

RDF (Resource Description Framework): A standard model for data interchange on the Web and a framework for constructing logical languages that can work together in the Semantic Web. A way of using XML for data rather than just documents. RDF extends the linking structure of the Web to use URIs to name the relationship between things as well as the two ends of the link (this is usually referred to as a "triple"). Using this simple model, it allows structured and semi-structured data to be mixed, exposed and shared across different applications (W3C, 1999).

Representation Data that encodes information about resource state (W3C, 2004a).

Resource Anything that might be identified by a URI (W3C, 2004a).

Semantic Concerned with the specification of meanings. Often contrasted with *syntactic* to emphasise the distinction between expressions and what they denote (W3C, 2004c).

Semantic Web The Web of data with meaning in the sense that a computer program can learn enough about what the data means to process it. Thus, a system that enables machines to understand and respond to complex human requests based on their meaning (Gruber, 2008; W3C, 1999).

Server A program that provides a service (typically information) to another program, called the client. A Web server holds Web pages and allows client programs to read and write them (W3C, 1999).

SIOC (Semantically Interlinked Online Communities): A Semantic Web ontology for representing rich data from the Social Web in RDF. It is commonly used in conjunction with the FOAF vocabulary for expressing personal profile and social networking information (DERI, 2011).

Social software Applications that include communication tools and interactive tools. Communication tools typically handle the capturing, storing and presentation of communication, usually written but increasingly including audio and video as well. Interactive tools handle mediated interactions between a pair or group of users. They focus on establishing and maintaining a connection among users, facilitating the mechanics of conversation and talk (Breslin et al., 2009).

Social Semantic Web Explicit and semantically rich knowledge representations created by social interactions on the Web (Gruber, 2008).

Social Web A set of social relations that link people through the Web (Gruber, 2008).

SSO (Single Sign-On): A property of access control of multiple related, but independent software systems. With this property a user logs in once and gains access to all systems without being prompted to log in again at each of them. As different applications and resources support different authentication mechanisms, single sign-on has to internally translate to and store different credentials compared to what is used for initial authentication (The Open Group, 2010).

Tag Descriptive markup delimiting the start and end (including its generic identifier and any attributes) of an element (W3C, 2001).

URI (Uniform Resource Identifier): The string (often starting with http:) that is used to identify anything on the Web (W3C, 1999).

URL (Uniform Resource Locator): A term used sometimes for certain URIs to indicate that they might change (W3C, 1999).

Widget A small program embedded in a graphical user interface, in kind of a framework or widget engine (W3, 2011).

WWW (World Wide Web): An information space in which items of interest are identified by URIs (W3C, 2004a).

XML (Extensible Markup Language): W3C's generic language for creating new markup languages (W3C, 1999).

References

Breslin, J., Passant, A., & Decker, S. (2009). *The Social Semantic Web*. Berlin: Springer.

Brusilovsky, P. (1996). Methods and techniques of adaptive hypermedia. *Journal of User Modelling and User Adaptation Interaction, 6*, 87–129.

Brusilovsky, P. (1998). Adaptive educational systems on the World-Wide-Web. In: Ayala G (Ed.), *Current trends and applications of artificial intelligence in education* (pp. 9–16). Proceedings of Workshop at the 4th World Congress on Expert Systems, ITESM, Mexico City, Mexico.

Clancey, W. J. (1985). Heuristic classification. *Artificial Intelligence, 27*, 289–350.

Coates, T. (2003) *On permalinks and paradigms*. Plasticbag. Retrieved December 5, 2011 from http://www.plasticbag.org/archives/2003/06/on_permalinks_and_paradigms/

DERI - Digital Enterprise Research Institute G. (2011). *SIOC-project.org*. Retrieved May 29, 2009 from http://sioc-project.org/

European Commission. (2002). *European report on quality indicators of lifelong learning*. Brussels: European Commission.

European Commission. (2008). *ALPINE - Adult Learning Professions in Europe: A study of the current situation, trends and issues*. Brussels: European Commission.

European Commission's Directorate-General for Education and Culture. (2011). Glossary of eLearning. Retrieved December 5, 2011 from http://www.elearningeuropa.info/en/glossary

FOAF Project. (2011). *The Friend of a Friend project*. Retrieved December 5, 2011 from http://www.foaf-project.org

Graf, S., Lan, C. H., Liu, T. C., & Kinshuk. (2009). Investigations about the effects and effectiveness of adaptivity for students with different learning styles. In *Proceedings of the IEEE International Conference on Advanced Learning Technologies* (ICALT 2009) (pp. 415–419). IEEE Computer Society Press, Los Alamitos, CA.

Gruber, T. (2008). Collective knowledge intelligence: Where the Social Web meets the Semantic Web. *Web Semantics: Science, Services and Agents on the World Wide Web, 6*, 4–13.

IEEE. (2000). *IEEE 100–2000. The authoritative dictionary of IEEE standards terms* (7th ed.). New York: IEEE Computer Society.

Jasig. (2011). *CAS*. Retrieved December 5, 2011 from http://www.jasig.org/cas

Leone, S. (2009). *PLE: A brick in the construction of a lifelong learning society. Technology supported environment for personalised learning methods and case studies*. Hershey, PA: IGI Global.

Leone, S. (2010). *F2F learning vs eLearning: the lifelong learner's point of view*. In Proceedings of INTED 2010.

MOAT-project.org. (2011). *MOAT: Meaning Of A Tag*. Retrieved December 5, 2011 from http://moat-project.org/

S. Leone, *Characterisation of a Personal Learning Environment as a Lifelong Learning Tool*, SpringerBriefs in Education, DOI 10.1007/978-1-4614-6274-3,
© Springer Science+Business Media New York 2013

Newell, A., & Simon, H. A. (1976). Computer science as empirical inquiry—Symbols and search. *Communications of the ACM, 19*, 113–126.

OASIS. (2011). *ODF*. Retrieved December 5, 2011 from http://opendocument.xml.org/

Oppermann, R. (1994). Introduction. In R. Oppermann (Ed.), *Adaptive user support: Ergonomic design of manually and automatically adaptable software* (pp. 1–13). Hillsdale, NJ: Lawrence Erlbaum Associates.

The Open Group. (2010). *Introduction to single sign-on*. Retrieved December 5, 2011 from http://www.opengroup.org/security/sso/sso_intro.htm

The PHP Group. (2011). *PHP*. Retrieved December 5, 2011 from http://www.php.net/

UNESCO. (1999). *The world declaration on higher education for the twenty-first century: Vision and action*. Paris: UNESCO

UNESCO Institute for Education. (1999). *Glossary of adult learning in Europe*. Paris: UNESCO.

W3C. (1995). *Hypertext terms*. Retrieved December 5, 2011 from http://www.w3.org/Terms

W3C. (1999). *Glossary of "Weaving the Web."* Retrieved December 5, 2011 from http://www.w3.org/People/Berners-Lee/Weaving/glossary.html

W3C. (2000). *Authoring tool accessibility Guidelines 1.0*. Retrieved December 5, 2011 from http://www.w3.org/TR/ATAG10

W3C. (2001). *Modularization of XHTML*. Retrieved December 5, 2011 from http://www.w3.org/TR/xhtml-modularization

W3C. (2004a). *Architecture of the World Wide Web* (Vol. 1). Retrieved December 5, 2011 from http://www.w3.org/TR/webarch/

W3C. (2004b). *OWL Web ontology language guide*. Retrieved December 5, 2011 from http://www.w3.org/TR/owl-guide/

W3C. (2004c). *RDF semantics*. Retrieved December 5, 2011 from http://www.w3.org/TR/rdf-mt/

W3C. (2004d). *Web services glossary*. Retrieved December 5, 2011 from http://www.w3.org/TR/ws-gloss/

W3C. (2004e). *Composite capability/preference profiles (CC/PP): Structure and vocabularies 1.0*. Retrieved December 5, 2011 from http://www.w3.org/TR/CCPP-struct-vocab/

W3C. (2005). *Glossary of terms for device independence*. Retrieved December 5, 2011 from http://www.w3.org/TR/di-gloss/

W3C. (2011). *Widget packaging and XML configuration*. Retrieved December 5, 2011 from http://www.w3.org/TR/widgets/